DEAD SOULS

A Comic Epic in Two Parts
Based on the Novel by Nikolay Gogol

Laurence Senelick

BROADWAY PLAY PUBLISHING INC
New York
www.broadwayplaypublishing.com
info@broadwayplaypublishing.com

DEAD SOULS
© Copyright 1984 Laurence Senelick

All rights reserved. This work is fully protected under the copyright laws of the United States of America. No part of this publication may be photocopied, reproduced, stored in a retrieval system, or transmitted, in any form or by any means, electronic, mechanical, recording, or otherwise, without the prior permission of the publisher. Additional copies of this play are available from the publisher.

Written permission is required for live performance of any sort. This includes readings, cuttings, scenes, and excerpts. For amateur and stock performances, please contact Broadway Play Publishing Inc. For all other rights please contact Laurence Senelick, 117 Mystic St, West Medford, MA 02155.

Cover art by William Sloane / THREE

First edition: May 1984
This edition: October 2017
I S B N: 978-0-88145-016-3

Book design: Marie Donovan
Typeface: Palatino & Baskerville by L & F Technical Composition, Lakeland, FL

First Performance Information

Dead Souls received its first production at the Tufts Arena Theatre, Medford, Massachusetts, on May 4-8 1982. It was directed by Laurence Senelick, with costume designs by Jan Fox and set design by Carroll R. Durand. The production was cited by the Boston critics as one of the season's ten best shows. The original cast, in alphabetical order, included:

Hank Azaria	Mizhuev; Cavalry Captain; Rural Police Captain; Putrefactov; Secretary at State Board of Guardians
Lynn Coutant Bailey	Korobochka; Old Codger at Town Hall
Rick Barter	Manilov; First Peasant; Chichikov's Superior; Peasant with Log
John R. Bianchi	Luigi the Waiter; Postmaster; Plyushkin's Son
David Conroy	Petrushka; Maksim Telyatnikov; Sysoy Pafnutievich
Colette Corry	Lizanka Manilova; A Wench of Korobochka's; Korobochka's Horse
David Michael Flaxman	Second Peasant; Themistoclius Manilov; Proshka; Grigory Try-and-Get-There-But-You-Won't; Prince Chipkhaikhilidzay
Greg Taft Gerard	Sanitation Inspector; Uncle Mityay; Official at Town Hall
Dean Harrison	Wedge-bearded Peasant; Barouche Coachman; Corky Stepan; Dandruffsky
Curtis Houlihan	Nozdryov; Young Man with Shotgun Stickpin; Second Clerk; Popov
Charles Kurtz	Public Prosecutor; Old Lady in Barouche; Manilov's Steward
Jenny Langsam	Dapple-gray in Troika; Ball Guest
Kate Levy	Plyushkin; Ivan Antonovich; Chichikov's Father

John Marcus	"Recording Secretary," a Troika Horse; First Clerk; Guest at at-home; Lady with Blue Plume
Joy Martinello	Lady with White Plume; Barouche Horse; A Wench of Korobochka's; Guest at at-home
Mary Nolen	Pelageya; Elizabethus Sparrow; Peasant Wench
Minette Norman	Anna Grigorievna; Plyushkin's Daughter's Governess; Fetiniya
Cathi Ostroff	Sofiya Ivanovna; Landlady of Roadside Inn; Plyushkin's Wife; Midwife
Christopher C. Payton	Gogol (who also plays Inn Waiter, Urchin, Manilov's Tutor, Police Officer, Coucou the Frenchman, and Captain Kopeikin)
Oliver Platt	Sobakevich; Priest; Macdonald Carlovich
Andrew Polk	Selifan; The Governor
Phoebe Reeves	Sorrel Nag in Troika; Ball Guest
Bill Reichblum	Pavel Ivanovich Chichikov
Scott Roberts	Chief of Police; Porfiry; Mrs. Sobakevich; Avvakum Fyrov; Chichikov's Client
Justine Shapiro	Governor's Daughter; Guest at at-home; A Wench of Korobochka's
Laurie Stusser	Governor's Wife; Nozdryov's Stallion; Plyushkin's Daughter
Gregory Tartaglia	Chief of Administrative Bureau; Alcides Manilov; Uncle Minyay
Gwen Waltz	Mavra; Uncle Mikhey; Footman; Chichikov's Schoolmaster

The action takes place in Rome and various regions of Gogol's imagination in the 1830s.

Production Note

This adaptation of *Dead Souls* differs from earlier versions in its attempt to integrate the narrator, or, more specifically, the character of Gogol into the action. Gogol intended *Dead Souls* to be the first part of a trilogy, presenting the ghastliness and squalor of the Russian soul to be redeemed and reclaimed to human worth and dignity in the later sections. He never completed the latter parts, but in the extant novel, the Inferno to his *Divine Comedy*, Gogol, as narrator, signals this potential development. His asides, reflections, second thoughts alert the audience to the deeper meaning of the comic details. His so-called "lyrical digressions" and extended metaphors present an idealized world of conventional sentiment and childlike innocence, to contrast with the sordid banality of the world in which his hero Chichikov moves. Without Gogol, *Dead Souls* loses much of its resonance and meaning. With Gogol, another dimension is added to the satiric characters and action.

Dead Souls is neither a socially committed attack on serfdom nor a realistic portrayal of Russian life. It is a virtuoso display of creativity by a master of improvisation. Gogol imbues his characters with his own ability to create, enabling them to interrupt him, tell their own anecdotes, and impute identities to other characters. The work is a verbal construct, and when the details and linguistic trickery are pared away, the magician's sleeve is shown to be empty. Therefore, in this dramatization, the sense of "performance" must be preserved, the performance of an author inventing before our eyes characters and situations which possess only as much substantiality as the imagination can bestow on them.

By putting Gogol the creator at the center of the play, I have tried to indicate that his Russia is an imaginary landscape. Gogol himself plays several roles in the story and can be utilized as a kind of all-purpose stagehand in setting the scene and providing props. The most important feeling to be conveyed is that Gogol is making it up as he goes along. Consequently, there must be an improvisational air to the way scenes and characters are brought on stage, a constant element of surprise and ingenuity. The action must move uninterruptedly, almost as in a dream. It should never become one of those tedious sequences of *tableaux vivants* that so often compose a dramatized novel. In this way, the presentation can become more theatrically adventurous and surrealistic, and revelation of Chichikov's past can, as in the novel, be left to the end, where it belongs.

Although this adaptation involves over a hundred characters, the cast need be no larger than fifteen, depending on the talents and versatility of the company. In the original production, staged at the Tufts Arena Theatre in May 1982, twenty-eight actors played all the roles, including the horses. Only Chichikov was played by an actor who never varied his identity. Sexual cross-casting is most desirable: Plyushkin has been successfully played by a woman; and in other productions, a male Korobochka might prove interesting. The doubling suggested in the First Performance Information indicates possible distribution of roles.

A basic feature of the production was quick change: the same items of clothing, makeup, set pieces would, like the actor, change identities and owners, often making a critical statement about the situation. For instance, there was a series of blank chairs which were given different backs depending on the personality of their owner. The drinks table on which the Public Prosecutor collapsed became his bier and he was carried to the cemetery on its removable top. This involved considerable coordination backstage but the result was well worth it.

The horses were essentially peasant men and women, whose long hair equalled manes, and who stood upright, but whose tails were of tow. Only the elaborate mime of their faces, legs, and feet defined their equine nature, and even then it was the horsiness of humanity or the humanity of these particular steeds that was stressed.

LAURENCE SENELICK

Guide to Pronunciation

This table is meant only as an approximation of the correct pronunciation of the Russian names. In the phonetic spellings, 'h should be pronounced by swallowing on the sound "h", "ay" should be pronounced as in "day", and "eye" should be pronounced as in "eyesore". Stress the capitalized syllable. The names are listed in the order in which they appear in the script.

Pushkin	POOSH-keen
Gogol	GAW-g'l
brichka	BREECH-kah
Kazan	kah-ZAHN
Petrushka	pit-ROOSH-kah
Selifan	syeh-lee-FAHN
Pavel Ivanovich Chichikov	POW'l ee-VAH-naw-veech TCHEE-tchee-kawff
Kotzebue	KAHT-zeh-boo-ay
Poplyovin	pahp-LYAW-veen
Zyablova	ZYAHB-lah-vah
Ivan Andreevich	ee-VAHN ahn-DRAY-ehveech
Ivan Andreich	ee-VAHN ahn-DRAYTCH
Zhukovsky	zhoo-KAWFF-skuy
Lyudmila	lyood-MEE-lah
Anton Antonovich Manilov	ahn-TAWN ahn-TAWN-ahveech mah-NEE-lawff
Mikhail Semyonovich Sobakevich	mih-'ha-YEEL Sem-YAWN-ah-veech sah-bahk-YAY-veech
Nozdryov	nahzd-RYAWFF
Mizhuev	mih-ZHOO-yehff
Potseluev	paht-sehl-LOO-yehff
Kuvshinikov	koov-SHEEN-ee-kawff
Manilovka	mah-NEE-lawff-kah
Zamanilovka	zah-mah-NEE-lawff-kah
Lizanka	LEE-zahn-kah
Kuechelgarten	KIH-'hel-GAHR-ten

Alcides	ahl-SEYE-deez
Themistoclius	them-iss-TAWK-lee-us
Fetiniya	feh-TEEN-yah
Nastasya Petrovna Korobochka	nahss-TAHSS-yah pit-RAWV-nah kah-RAH-bahch-kah
Pelageya	pil-lah-GAY-ah
Porfiry	pawr-FEE-ree
Maksimov	mahk-SEE-mawff
Andryushka	ahn-DRYOOSH-kah
Mityay	meet-YAY
Minyay	meen-YAY
Feoduliya Ivanovna	fay-ah-DOO-lee-yah ee-VAH-nahff-nah
Mikheyev	mee-'HAY-yehff
Stepan	stih-PAHN
Milushkin	MEE-loosh-keen
Maksim Telyatnikov	mahk-SEEM tehl-YAHT-nee-kawff
Plyushkin	PLYOOSH-keen
Proshka	PRAWSH-kah
Mavra	MAHV-rah
Pyotr	PYAWT-r
Mikhey	mih-'HAY
Grigory	grih-GAW-ruy
Popov	PAW-pahff
Ivan Ivanovich Ivanov	ee-VAHN ee-VAHN-ah-veech ee-VAHN-awff
Oryol	ahr-YAWL
Antip Prokhorov	ahn-TEEP PRAW-'hah-rawff
Avvakum Fyrov	ah-vah-KOOM FEE-rawff
Feodosey Feodosyev	fyeh-ah-DAW-say fyeh-ah-DAW-syehff
Ivan Antonovich	ee-VAHN ahn-TAWN-ah-veech
Kherson	'HYEHR-sahn
Fyodor Fyodorovich Perekroev	FYAW-dahr FYAW-dah-rah-veech pyeh-reh-KRAW-yehff
Ryazan	ryah-ZAHN
Simbirsk	seem-BEERSK

GUIDE TO PRONUNCIATION

Sofron Ivanovich Bezpechny	shaf-RAWN ee-VAHN-ah-veech byehz-PYECH-nuy
Adelaida	ah-dyeh-lah-EE-da
Mariya Gavrilovna	mah-REE-yah gav-REE-lawff-nah
Aleksandra Gavrilovna	ah-lyehk-SAHN-drah gav-REE-lawff-nah
Adelheida Gavrilovna	ah-dyehl-HEYE-dah gav-REE-lawff-nah
Katerina Mikhailovna	kah-tyeh-REE-nah mih-'HEYE-lawff-nah
Rosa Fyodorovna	Raw-zah FYAW-dah-rawff-nah
Emilia Fyodorovna	eh-MEE-lee-yah FYAW-dah-rawff-nah
Frol Vasilievich Pobedonosov	FRAWL vah-SEEL-yay-veech pah-byeh-dah-NAW-sawff
Pyotr Vasilievich	PYAWT-r vah-SEEL-yay-veech
Pyotr Varsonofievich	PYAWT-r vahr-sahn-AWFF-yay-veech
Pelageya Egorovna	pih-lah-GAY-ah yeh-GAWR-awff-nah
Sofia Rostislavna	SAW-fyah rahs-tih-SLAHF-nah
Sofia Aleksandrovna	SAW-fyah ah-lyehk-SAHN-drawff-nah
Praskoviya Fyodorovna	prahs-KAWFF-yah FYAW-dah-rawff-nah
Anna Grigorievna	AH-nah gree-GAWR-yehff-nah
Sofiya Ivanovna	SAW-fyah ee-VAHN-awff-nah
Antipatr	ahn-tee-PAHT-r
Sysoy Pafnutievich	sih-SOY pahf-NOOT-yeh-veech
Odnozorovsky-Chementinsky	ahd-nah-ZAW-rahff-skuy-cheh-myehn-TEEN-skuy

Kopeikin	kah-PYAY-keen
Krasny	KRAHSS-nuy
Ryazan	ryah-ZAHN
Mikhailo	mih-'HEYE-lah
Sidor	SEE-dahr
Vakhramey	va'h-rah-MAY
Derebin	dihr-YAY-been
Perependev	pyeh-ryeh-PYEHN-dyehff
Pavlusha	pahv-LYOOSH-ah
Pavlushka	pahv-LYOOSH-kah

PART ONE

Episode 1

(*Rome on a bright sunny day. Mandolin music is playing in the background.* GOGOL *is seated at a café table, with a demi-tasse before him.*)

LUIGI: Più di caffè, signore?

GOGOL: Si, Luigi.

LUIGI: (*Pouring.*) The Signor Gogol like his macaroni?

GOGOL: Very much, Luigi. When I get back to St. Pete, I intend to invite in all my friends and prepare it for them. What cheeses do you use?

LUIGI: Is *misto*, signore: a little parmigiano, a little romano, some goat cheese from the mountains.

GOGOL: Aha. Well, I shall have to improvise. Improvisation is something I'm very good at. Tell me, who's your favorite author?

LUIGI: Dante, Signor Gogol.

GOGOL: I love Rome! Even the waiters are literary! I can't imagine a waiter at an inn in Moscow knowing who Pushkin was.

LUIGI: And who is this Signor Pushpin, signore?

GOGOL: He *was* Russia's greatest writer. But he's gone now. And I intend to be Russia's greatest writer. It's a terrific responsibility, one must be the conscience of a whole nation, but I shall endure it. A grappa, per favore!

LUIGI: Subito! (*Bringing the drink.*) Did Signor Pushpin write poem like *La Divina commedia*?

GOGOL: No, Luigi mio, but *I* shall. I have conceived a story, with its own Inferno, Purgatorio, and Paradiso.

LUIGI: Prima, signore!

GOGOL: Unfortunately, somehow I can't seem to get myself out of Hell. (*He takes out a cheroot.*)

LUIGI: (*Lighting it.*) What is called your poem, signore?

GOGOL: Dead souls.

LUIGI: Ah, *ma che orrore!* (*Crosses himself.*) The Church, she say no soul can die. All soul is *immortale*.

GOGOL: Our Orthodox Church says the same thing. But in our benighted country, Luigi, souls can mean serfs. (LUIGI *shrugs.*) Serfs, slaves, *schiavi*. We Russians are slave-owning Slavs. And dead souls are those deceased peasants who must be crossed off the census rolls at the end of each year, so their owners don't have to pay tax on them any more.

LUIGI: It sound ver' *morbiddo*. You write a *tragedia* about peasants?

GOGOL: No, no, this is to be a comic epic, this Hell part. Eventually, in the later sections, the other dead souls — the living whose souls are dormant — will awake, and then Paradise will come to pass.

LUIGI: (*Losing interest.*) I clear away now, signore?

GOGOL: Fine, fine. You must show me how to make this stuff next time I'm in. Hold on! Look at this tubular bit of pasta.

LUIGI: Rigatoni.

GOGOL: It's a zero, a blank to be filled in, like my leading character. A hero who is a zero. And it rolls along the table like a carriage wheel. Imagine a carriage driving into a provincial town on two rounds.

LUIGI: Of rigatoni?

GOGOL: No, two round wheels. A smartish sort of brichka. . . .

LUIGI: Ma ch'e cosa, signore?

Episode 2

GOGOL: A brichka, a light travelling carriage, drawn by a troika — that's a team of three horses. The kind of carriage favored by gentry of the run-of-the-mill variety. There's a gent seated in the carriage — no fashion plate, but no eyesore either — neither too young or too old, too stout or too thin. And his arrival creates no stir, for it is noticed only by a couple of peasants idling by the roadside.

(*During this speech,* CHICHIKOV'S *brichka has entered, driven by* SELIFAN, *with* PETRUSHKA *curled up at the back. The bright Roman day has darkened into a Russian afternoon. Balalaika music briefly swells up, then dies out.*)

FIRST PEASANT: Looky there now! That's what I calls a wheel! What d'ye think? Would that there wheel make it to Moscow or not?

SECOND PEASANT: It'd make it all right.

FIRST PEASANT: But not so far as Kazan, I'll betcha?

SECOND PEASANT: Not so far's Kazan no ways.

GOGOL: As the carriage drove up to the inn it met with a young man in white dimity trousers and a swallowtail coat, making a brave stab at fashion, his dickey fastened by a cheap bronze stickpin in the shape of a pistol. The young man turned around, looked the vehicle over while clutching his cap which the wind had almost blown off, and then went away, never to be heard of in this story again.

(*A* YOUNG MAN *has indeed gone through those motions. A lively* INN SERVANT *rushes up to take the occupant of the brichka to his room.*)

INN SERVANT: (*Who is* GOGOL, *having taken a napkin from the Italian waiter.*) The chamber that God had provided the gentleman was a familiar sort, where for two rubles a day transients are provided with a restful bedroom with cockroaches peeking out of every corner like raisins in a pudding. While the transient gentleman inspected his room, his belongings were carried in.

(SELIFAN *and* PETRUSHKA *bring in a small white trunk, a small mahogany casket, a pair of shoetrees, and a roast chicken wrapped in blue paper.*)

INN SERVANT: Petruska the flunky was by temperament taciturn rather than talkative and had two characteristic traits: He would read whatever came under his nose, for it was the very process of reading pleased him—lo and behold, some word or other would emerge from the welter of letters, although the Devil alone knew what the word meant.

PETRUSHKA: (*Reading.*) It-was-a-dark-and-stor-my-nig-hit.

GOGOL: Secondly, he had a peculiar atmosphere of his own, redolent of lived-in quarters, so that all he had to do was set up his cot and drag in his overcoat, and it would seem as if people had been living there for ten years or so.

CHICHIKOV: What the hell's wrong with you, boy? You're sweating or something. Go and take a bath, at least.

PETRUSHKA: (*To himself, as he tidies up his master's things.*) Don't you get bored saying the same thing over and over again. . . .

INN SERVANT: Selifan the coachman was an altogether different sort of man. . . . (SELIFAN *steps forward.*) But the author is quite conscience-stricken taking up your time with persons of the lower classes. (SELIFAN *is disgruntled.*) He knows you much prefer scraping an acquaintance with individuals who are but a single step above you in rank.

SELIFAN: I'll go see to the horses.

INN SERVANT: Meanwhile, the gentleman descended to the common room, the usual common room with the same sooty ceiling, the same smoke-blotched chandelier and the same picture of a nymph with such enormous breasts that, I'm sure, none of you has ever seen the like.

Episode 2

CHICHIKOV: Dinner!

INN SERVANT: (*Serving*.) Cabbage soup with dumplings (we keep 'em for weeks at a time for the special benefit of travellers), brains with peas, sausages and sauerkraut, roast chicken, dill pickles, and layer cake.

CHICHIKOV: (*Tucking in.*) Tell me, waiter, does this inn do a good business?

INN SERVANT: So, so, sir.

CHICHIKOV: And the owner, is he an honest man?

INN SERVANT: Oh, a real crook, sir.

CHICHIKOV: Tell me now, the Governor . . .

GOGOL: And so he inquired with great particularity about all the officials in the town and especially the landowners: how many souls each one owned, how far out of town he lived—and what diseases and epidemic fevers were prevalent.

CHICHIKOV: (*Blows his nose. A trumpet sounds.*)

INN SERVANT: (*Stands up straight.*) Was there somethin' else wantin', sir?

CHICHIKOV: I believe the police department requires the name of all strangers. Here is my card.

INN SERVANT: "Collegiate Councilor Pavel Ivanovich Chichikov, landowner, travelling on private business." (*Another trumpet sneeze.*)

GOGOL: After dinner, he strolled around the town, reading the signboards. (*Held up by* GOGOL.)

CHICHIKOV: "Liquors at Retail," "This way to the Academy,"—ah, a bill of the play. "The Virgin of the Sun" by August Kotzebue, Rollo Mr. Poplyovin, Cora Mlle. Zyablova, hmm, hmm, parterre two rubles, hm, hmm, Printed by the Provincial Administrative press." Some trash about Incas, I suppose. (*Takes down the poster, folds it up and slips it in his pocket.*)

GOGOL: And the day was brought to a close by cold veal, borscht, and slumber, with the air-pumps going full blast. He slept well as if troubled by neither hemorrhoids or a conscience. (CHICHIKOV's *snores also produced by musical instrument.*) The next day was devoted to paying calls on the local officials. The Governor. . . . (GOGOL *activates each character by putting a costume item, a prop, a wig or nose on him.*)

Episode 3

GOVERNOR: You must excuse me, I was in the middle of my embroidery. (*Shows an embroidery frame.*)

CHICHIKOV: Your excellency, driving into your province is like driving into paradise. The roads are so smooth they seem lined with velvet. Governments that appoint such wise functionaries are deserving of much praise.

GOVERNOR: How kind of you. Really, you must come to a little at-home I'm having tonight.

GOGOL: The Chief of the Administrative Bureau.

CHICHIKOV: Pleased to meet you, Your Excellency.

BUREAU CHIEF: I'm not an Excellency, I'm only an Honor.

CHICHIKOV: *Only* an Honor! Most sorry, Your Excell—— I mean, your Honor.

BUREAU CHIEF: Come and play cards some time.

GOGOL: The Chief of Police.

CHICHIKOV: I really must commend you on the vigilance of your men. While I was out walking last night, I was struck by the alertness of the policemen on duty.

CHIEF OF POLICE: You don't say so? We ought to have dinner soon.

CHICHIKOV: Delighted.

GOGOL: The Public Prosecutor.

Episode 3

CHICHIKOV: Me, why I'm just an insignificant worm, though I've had to suffer much in my day in the service of my country. I have all sorts of enemies, they've even made attempts on my life, but now, desirous of peace and quiet, I think I have found in this town a place to settle down.

PUBLIC PROSECUTOR: (*Dosing himself with medicine.*) Very plausible. A cup of tea?

GOGOL: The Postmaster.

CHICHIKOV: I'm please . . .

POSTMASTER: (*At a breathless clip.*) Do call me Ivan Andreevich, won't you, although around here they always refer me to as Ivan Andreich-Sprechen-Sie-Deutsch, just their little joke, so to speak, because I go in for philosophy and burn the midnight oil over Young's *Night Thoughts*, have you read it, my dear sir? Well just imagine, the Bureau Chief himself is a poetry lover, knows Zhukovsky's *Lyudmila* by heart, you might say, and recites it beautifully, why when he gets to "Hush!" he says it in such a way you can actually sort of see the dale slumbering, you know.

BUREAU CHIEF and POSTMASTER: (*In unison, with oratorial gestures.*) "Sleeps the pine-grove; the dale slumbers. Hush!"

CHICHIKOV: Do tell.

POSTMASTER: See you tonight.

GOGOL: The preparation for the Governor's at-home took over two hours, for the newcomer displayed a carefulness in grooming quite out of the ordinary.

CHICHIKOV: (*Scrubs his cheeks, puffing them out; wipes his face, starting with the back of his ears; takes a towel from* INN SERVANT*'s shoulder, and snorts in his face; puts on a dickey, plucks his nose hairs, and dons a cranberry-colored coat.*)

(*During this the music of the at-home has begun in a very subdued manner.*) (*A low buzz begins as the guests gather and the lights come up.*)

GOGOL: (*Becoming a party guest.*) Have you ever seen flies flit over a gleaming white loaf of sugar on a sultry July day, as an old housekeeper stands at an open window, dividing it into glittering, irregular lumps; a flock of children look on curiously as her aged hands lift the hammer, while the aerial squadrons of flies, upheld by the buoyant air, boldly dart in as if they owned the place and taking advantage of the blinding sunlight, bestrew the dainty morsels, rubbing their legs against each other or scratching under their gossamer wings.

(*The hovering cluster of flies breaks up and becomes the officials and their wives. A blaze of light.* CHICHIKOV's *hand is seized by the* GOVERNOR.)

GOVERNOR: Pavel Ivanovich, so good of you to come! Allow me to introduce you to my wife. (*Exchange of greetings with* GOVERNOR'S WIFE.)

CHICHIKOV: I am charmed to make the acquaintance of a lady whose graces are known to fame even beyond the frontiers of this province.

GOVERNOR'S WIFE: (*Simpers.*) Too kind!

POSTMASTER: Ah, Pavel Ivanovich, I'm sorry to interrupt, but do come and join us in a game of whist. We've been waiting for you with bated breath, so to speak.

CHICHIKOV: By all means.

(*The* CHIEF OF POLICE, PUBLIC PROSECUTOR, SANITATION INSPECTOR, *and* BUREAU CHIEF *are already playing cards.* MANILOV *is kibitzing.*)

SANITATION INSPECTOR: Here's a spady-lady, a spadel-adel'll make the gradel.

BUREAU CHIEF: (*Slamming down a king.*) Go on, you backwoods yokel! I'll knock off your moustache for you!

PUBLIC PROSECUTOR: Come what may—if there's nothing else, then play diamonds!

CHIEF OF POLICE: (*Playing a queen.*) Get out of my hand, you old bag!

MANILOV: (*Rising.*) I don't believe we've yet been introduced.

EPISODE 3

POSTMASTER: Collegiate Councilor Pavel Ivanovich Chichikov, this is Anton Antonvich Manilov, one of our local landowners.

CHICHIKOV: (*Having bowed affably to the company.*) I have been longing to make your acquaintance. (*They freeze.*)

GOGOL: God alone, perhaps, could tell what Manilov's character was like. There is a species of man labelled, as the proverb puts it, "neither fish nor flesh nor good red herring." During the first minute or so of a conversation with him you could not help but say, "What a pleasant, kind-hearted man!" The next minute you would not say anthing at all, while the third minute you would say, "What the hell is going on!" (*The freeze is broken.*)

MANILOV: Really, we must have a little talk. Please, Ivan Andreich, take my hand for a round or two. (*He and* CHICHIKOV *move away.*)

CHIEF OF POLICE: Don't monopolize our Pavel Ivanovich for too long, now!

MANILOV: (*To* CHICHIKOV.) How do you like our town? Are you having a good time?

CHICHIKOV: A splendid town, really first-rate, and I am having a wonderful time.

MANILOV: And what do you think of our host, the Governor? A most estimable and agreeable man, isn't he?

CHICHIKOV: Perfectly true, most estimable. And how he puts his heart into his work.

MANILOV: I know what you mean. He just showed me a beaded purse he was finishing!

CHICHIKOV: There ought to be more people like him!

MANILOV: And the Bureau Chief, isn't he well informed and intelligent?

CHICHIKOV: (*Restless.*) Absolutely.

MANILOV: And what's your opinion of the Chief of Police?

CHICHIKOV: (*Taking over the conversation.*) A sweetheart. Tell me, do you spend all your time in the country?

MANILOV: Alas.

CHICHIKOV: You must get bored out on your estate all the time.

MANILOV: For the most part. Leading a cloistered life, you start to vegetate and have to come to town just to meet educated people.

CHICHIKOV: How true.

MANILOV: Of course, if we had some decent neighbors with whom we could chat about the niceties of grammar or modern science, some topic that would lend wings to the soul, then village life and solitude would have their advantages. . . .

CHICHIKOV: How true.

MANILOV: But as it is, all a person can do is dip into the Moscow papers now and then.

CHICHIKOV: You amaze me! What could be more gratifying than to view Mother Nature's gaudy pageant and read a book once in a while.

MANILOV: But, without a friend to share it . . .

CHICHIKOV: How true! What good are all the treasures in the world! "Hoard not gold, but a good friend hold!" as the proverb says.

MANILOV: (*His face becoming cloyingly saccharine.*) You know, Pavel Ivanovich, when one has a friend, one feels a sort of spiritual . . . delectation, in a manner of speaking. For instance, now, when fate has afforded me the rare—I may even say, unique—happiness of enjoying your pleasant conversation—

CHICHIKOV: Please, what pleasant conversation can I afford?

MANILOV: (*Clasping* CHICHIKOV*'s hand.*) Oh, Pavel Ivanovich, I would gladly give up half of what I own to have a fraction of your talents!

Episode 3

CHICHIKOV: (*Clasping him back.*) No, no, quite the contrary, I . . .

(*While frozen in this warm mutual clutch, they are interrupted and split up by some dancers coming through.*)

MANILOV: (*Overcome with emotion.*) Pavel Ivanovich . . . would you deign to honor my village . . . which is only about ten miles from town—with a visit? My wife and I would be so flattered . . . so happy . . . We could take tea on the veranda, philosophize in the shade of an elm tree . . . Will you . . . will you come?

CHICHIKOV: Indeed I will. For me it will be more than a pleasure, it will be a . . . sacred obligation.

POSTMASTER: (*From the card table.*) Pavel Ivanovich! Anton Antonovich! We're waiting!

CHICHIKOV: Do go in. I shall follow you.

MANILOV: No, Pavel Ivanovich, no—you're a stranger here.

CHICHIKOV: Don't put yourself out; please do go in.

MANILOV: I would never allow such a cultured guest to follow behind me!

CHICHIKOV: You have too high an opinion of my culture. After you!

MANILOV: I won't hear of it!

CHICHIKOV: I insist.

(*At the point where they are about to go together,* SOBAKEVICH *enters and treads heavily on* CHICHIKOV*'s foot.*)

CHICHIKOV: Oww!

MANILOV: (*Shocked.*) Mikhail Semyonovich, for shame!

SOBAKEVICH: All right, I know how it goes! Sobakevich is a bear, Sobakevich is a brute, out of place in fashionable drawing-rooms.

MANILOV: I didn't say that, Mikhail Semyonovich. You're . . . you're exaggerating . . .

SOBAKEVICH: (*Shrugs; to* CHICHIKOV.) Not too much damage, I hope?

CHICHIKOV: (*Who has brightened up at the name Sobakevich.*) Not at all . . . In fact, I bless this accident for bringing me into contact with . . . (*Pause.*) I've heard a good deal about you, Mikhail Semyonovich.

SOBAKEVICH: I can imagine. (*Slaps* MANILOV *on the back.*)

CHICHIKOV: (*To* MANILOV.) My dear friend, may I abuse your kindness by asking you to tell our friends that . . . I shall join them presently?

MANILOV: Why . . . of course. (*He goes off in some bewilderment.*) (*Others freeze.*)

GOGOL: As everyone knows, there are some faces that Nature does not spend much thought or ingenuity on, not using delicate tools like files or chisels, but simply hacks out with a full swipe of the axe: one swipe, there's the nose; another swipe, there's the lips, and without wasting time on polishing or trimming, she sends her handiwork into the world, saying "It lives!" Such was Sobakevich's. (*End of freeze.*)

SOBAKEVICH: (*Looking back after* MANILOV.) To think that pantywaist owns three hundred souls! Holy saints!

CHICHIKOV: Yes, I realize you're a man of more sober interests. The Bureau Chief was telling me the other day . . . Isn't he a splendid fellow!

SOBAKEVICH: Who?

CHICHIKOV: The Bureau Chief.

SOBAKEVICH: The Bureau Chief? Why, he's the most perfect fool the world has yet produced.

CHICHIKOV: (*Taken aback.*) Of course, every man has his weaknesses. But the Governor now, what an excellent chap!

SOBAKEVICH: The Governor an excellent chap?

EPISODE 3

CHICHIKOV: Yes . . . isn't he?

SOBAKEVICH: A highway robber—biggest one on earth!

CHICHIKOV: A highway robber? I'd never think so to look at him. He seems so gentle, those purses he embroiders, his kindly face. . . . .

SOBAKEVICH: A highway robber's face! You put a knife in his hands and let him loose on the highway, and he'll slit your throat—slit it for a penny.

(*A* FOOTMAN *hands round hors d'oeuvres.* SOBAKEVICH *wolfs down plenty.* CHICHIKOV *is more delicate.*)

CHICHIKOV: But he provides such a good table for his guests. . . .

SOBAKEVICH: You know what the dishes are made out of?

CHICHIKOV: No, but I'm told the pork chops and stewed fish are excellent.

SOBAKEVICH: It just seems that way. The chef's a Frenchman: He'll skin a cat and serve it up as a rabbit.

CHICHIKOV: (*Spitting out an hors d'oeuvre he had just taken.*) Ugh, what a nasty thing to say!

SOBAKEVICH: That's how they do things. All sorts of garbage, stuff my cook throws into the cesspool, pardon my French, they pop into the soup. You can plaster frog's legs with sugar, so far as I'm concerned, and I won't touch 'em—and I won't eat oysters either. Oysters remind me of something I can't name in mixed company. It's all the fault of the Frenchies and the Krauts and their diets, ruining Russian stomachs. They're forever talking about education this and education that, but it's all just so much . . . flapdoodle! I'd use another word, but it's not polite in company. That's not my way. If it's mutton I want, then bring in the whole ram; and if it's pork send up the whole hog.

CHICHIKOV: (*Sighs.*) If only I had met a man of your common sense in my early days.

SOBAKEVICH: Listen, you, what's your name, Pavel Something, how about a visit to my place in the country?

CHICHIKOV: Why, Mikhail Semyonovich, I'd be . . .

SOBAKEVICH: Shake on it! That way you'll find out what a well-run estate looks like. And you can compare it with Manilov's

CHICHIKOV: Beg pardon?

SOBAKEVICH: You *did* get an invitation to Manilov's, didn't you?

(CHICHIKOV *is disconcerted.*)

POSTMASTER: Pavel Ivanovich, once and for all, so to speak, are you going to sit in at whist? It really isn't fair to let yourself be monopolized this way.

SOBAKEVICH: (*Departing.*) Enjoy yourself.

(ANNA GRIGORIEVNA *and* SOFIYA IVANOVNA *enter.*)

ANNA GRIGORIEVNA: Ah, there he is! Don't you dance, Pavel Ivanovich? I want to claim you for the next mazurka.

SOFIYA IVANOVNA: Spending all your time with the landowners, for shame! We ladies have rights too.

(NOZDRYOV *crashes in, tipsy, with* MIZHUEV *in tow.*)

NOZDRYOV: Who's calling for landowners? Ah, ladies, lovely ladies. (*He starts toward them but they disappear in a flurry, crying "Nozdryov, Nozdryov."*)

NOZDRYOV: Who're you? Oh yes, you must be that Chichikov they're all talking about. Is your name really Chichikov? Never mind, I don't stand on ceremony. . . . Guess where I'm coming from? The fair. Congratulate me, I lost my shirt, never had such a losing streak.

MIZHUEV: Yes you did.

NOZDRYOV: You know this fellow? This is my brother-in-law Mizhuev! We were talking about you all morning. "You just wait and see," says I, "if we don't meet this Chichikov." You know, if I had had another fifty rubles, I could have won back all my losses—put thirty thousand in my pocket.

MIZHUEV: Not true. I gave you fifty rubles and you lost them too.

EPISODE 3   15

NOZDRYOV: Never, never! You think that Major of yours is such a great player?

MIZHUEV: Good player or not, he fleeced you to a fare-thee-well.

NOZDRYOV: (*To Chichikov*.) Guess how much I lost! Four carriage-horses, my watch-chain, my watch, the lot! Ah, but did we have a time at the fair . . . when we started drinking, brother. . . . Cavalry Captain Potseluev, what a moustache, calls Bordeaux bordellos. "Bring us some bordellos!" he'll call. And that champagne! This stuff the Governor serves is swill in comparison. It wasn't Clicquot, it was some sort of Clicquot-Matradura, which means a super-Clicquot. Bouquet like a bunch of roses! Would you believe it, I personally drank seventeen bottles of it at one go!

MIZHUEV: You never.

NOZDRYOV: As I'm an honest man, I'm telling you I did drink that many.

MIZHUEV: You couldn't drink even ten.

NOZDRYOV: Want to make a bet?

MIZHUEV: Why bet on a thing like that?

NOZDRYOV: Bet me the gun you just bought.

MIZHUEV: I don't want to.

NOZDRYOV: 'Course not, you'd be out a gun. Ah, Chichikov, I'm sorry you weren't there. You and Lieutenant Kuvshinikov would have been like brothers. What a lech, won't let even peasant girls get by him. "Crawling on your belly for the strawberries," he calls it. Hey, Chichikov, why the hell didn't you come with us? You're a pig not to have come, you cattle-breeder you! Gimme a kiss, sweetheart, I'm really awfully fond of you.

(CHICHIKOV *has made an attempt to escape during this, and now a couple of footmen, prompted by the* GOVERNOR, *eject* NOZDRYOV, *followed by* MIZHUEV. CHICHIKOV *finally sits down at the card table.*)

CHICHIKOV: You are pleased to lead; I have the honor of trumping your deuce. Have some snuff.

GOGOL: And so the newcomer had a never-failing presence of mind and, whatever the conversation, showed himself to be an experienced man of the world. No matter which way you regarded him, he was a very decent fellow. (*The Officials sneeze in unison, having partaken of the snuff.*)

GOVERNOR: A well-intentioned person.

PUBLIC PROSECUTOR: A man of affairs.

CHIEF OF POLICE: Meritorious and amiable.

BUREAU CHIEF: *Experienced* and meritorious.

POSTMASTER: A learned man.

SOBAKEVICH: I like him.

GOGOL: That was the general opinion until such time as a certain strange enterprise the newcomer embarked on threw the whole town into utter bewilderment.

Episode 4

CHICHIKOV: Selifan, harness the horses! Petrushka, stay here and keep an eye on the room. (*Sniffs.*) What *have* you been doing? Give me a clove to put up my nose!

(CHICHIKOV *and* SELIFAN *get in the carriage and start out; a passing* PRIEST *doffs his hat. An* URCHIN (*played by* GOGOL) *tries to climb on the back. A Russian folktune has played during this sortie.*)

URCHIN: Kind sir, give something to a poor orphan!

(SELIFAN *flicks his whip at the* URCHIN *on the back, knocking him off.*)

GOGOL: Hardly was the town out of sight, when all sorts of claptrap and bushwah unfurled on either side: hillocks, fir stands, wild heather, and similar nonsense. Villages all strung out in a line, with peasants yawning on benches, women looking out of second-story windows and sows looking out of first-story windows. In short, the usual scenery.

EPISODE 4

CHICHIKOV: How many miles is it so far?

SELIFAN: Nigh on eleven, boss.

CHICHIKOV: Then where the devil is Manilov's place, where is Manilovka? Stop and ask somebody.

SELIFAN: (*To* PEASANT WITH WEDGE-SHAPED BEARD.) How far is it to Manilovka?

PEASANT WITH WEDGE-SHAPED BEARD: (*Doffs his hat.*) It's Manilovka you're wanting, not Zamanilovka?

SELIFAN: Manilovka, Manilovka.

PEASANT WITH WEDGE-SHAPED BEARD: Oh, Manilovka. Now you jest drive on for a mile or so an' you'll be there—sort of straight ahead to the right.

SELIFAN: To the right?

PEASANT WITH WEDGE-SHAPED BEARD: The right. That's your road to Manilovka; as for Zamanilovka, there ain't so sich a place nohow. This here's called Manilovka, but there ain't no Zamanilovka hereabouts at all. When you git there, you'll see a house up on a hill, stone one, two stories—the manor house, that is. That there's Manilovka; but as for Zamanilovka, there ain't so sich a place nohow hereabouts nor ain't never been.

(*During the latter part of this speech,* CHICHIKOV *and* SELIFAN *have moved on.*)

CHICHIKOV: When a friend invites you to visit his village, just ten miles out of town, it's bound to be a good twenty miles distant.

GOGOL: The village of Manilovka was far from alluring. The manor house stood on a bluff open to all the winds of heaven. The garden was in the English style: a pond covered with greenish scum and a small gazebo with an inscription reading, "A Temple for Solitary Meditation."

(MANILOV *appears with his* STEWARD. *He is meditatively puffing on a long pipe.*)

STEWARD: Master, it's about time we built that stone bridge over the pond, so's the peasants kin git acrost easy.

MANILOV: Yes, that's not a bad idea. Not a bad idea at all. And then, you know, if the bridge gets built, we could put shops on either side and have merchants sitting in the shops to sell the peasants all sorts of little necessities. Ah yes, I must think about that.

STEWARD: But we been talkin' about this bridge for going on two years now.

MANILOV: That's all right. I must give it some more thought. (*Spotting* CHICHIKOV.) Why, Pavel Ivanovich, you managed to remember us at last!

(*Kisses and embraces.* MANILOV *leads* CHICHIKOV *into the house.*)

GOGOL: Manilov's wife . . . however they were perfectly satisfied with one another.

LIZANKA: My darling, open your mouth and let me pop this pickled mushroom in it.

MANILOV: Lizanka, my love, do meet Pavel Ivanovich Chichikov.

LIZANKA: (*Lisping.*) How blissful you have made us by your coming! Not a day goes by when my husband doesn't mention your name.

MANILOV: Yes, she was always asking me, "Why doesn't your friend show up?" "Wait, sweetheart, he will." And so you are actually honoring us with a visit. How delightful . . . like a day in May . . . a birthday of the heart . . . Please stay for dinner, it isn't what you'd be offered on a parquet floor, but our humble fare comes from the heart . . .

CHICHIKOV: I would be enchanted.

MANILOV: (*As they proceed into the dining room.*) Don't sit on any of those chairs! They aren't finished yet!

(*Two little boys are already there. Their* TUTOR (GOGOL) *is tying napkins about their necks.*)

Episode 4

CHICHIKOV: What darling children! And how old might they be?

LIZANKA: The elder, Themistoclius, is eight, and the younger, Alcides, celebrated his sixth birthday just yesterday. And this is their tutor, Herr Kuechelgarten.

GOGOL: Guten Tag.

MANILOV: Themistoclius, which is the finest city in France?

THEMISTOCLIUS: Paris.

MANILOV: And what is our finest city?

THEMISTOCLIUS: Petersburg.

MANILOV: And the other one?

THEMISTOCLIUS: (*With prompting from the tutor.*) Mah . . . mah . . .

TUTOR: (*Whisper.*) Moscow.

THEMISTOCLIUS: (*Triumphant.*) Moo-Cow!

CHICHIKOV: What a clever little darling. So tender in years and yet so well-informed!

MANILOV: I intend to make a diplomat of him. Do you want to be an ambassador, Themistoclius?

THEMISTOCLIUS: (*His mouth full.*) I wanna.

LIZANKA: Please wipe the ambassador's nose.

(TUTOR *wipes* THEMISTOCLIUS' *nose.*) (*The dinner party fades out with the* MANILOVS *and* CHICHIKOV *conversing, vivaciously, the* TUTOR *smiling when they smile but rapping on the table to call the children to order; and* THEMISTOCLIUS *biting* ALCIDES' *ear.*)

LIZANKA: (*Fading in again.*) You haven't eaten a thing—

CHICHIKOV: Thank you—I'm full. Pleasant talk is better than any dish.

MANILOV: Then permit me to show you into my study. This is my den. Oh, permit me not to permit you to sit in any of those chairs either. They aren't finished. This is the guest armchair; guests have to sit here, like it or not. Permit me to offer you a small pipeful. . . .

CHICHIKOV: Permit me to decline. I don't smoke.

MANILOV: (*Regretfully.*) Permit me to inquire why not?

CHICHIKOV: Permit me to remark that pipe-smoking causes asthma.

MANILOV: Permit me to inform you that this is a prejudice. Why, I once knew a lieutenant . . . .

CHICHIKOV: Permit me to change the subject. (*Looks around cautiously.*) How long ago was it since you sent an inventory of your serfs to the Census Bureau?

MANILOV: Why, a good while ago; though to tell the truth, I can't recall.

CHICHIKOV: How many of your serfs have died since you last sent in an inventory?

MANILOV: I really can't say; I suppose I'd better ask my Steward. Steward! Step in here a minute. (STEWARD *enters, as if he had just got out of bed.*) Tell me, my man, how many of our folks died since the last census?

STEWARD: What do you mean, how many? Lots and lots and lots. (*Hiccups.*)

MANILOV: Just what I was thinking myself. Lots and lots—precisely! (*To* CHICHIKOV, *pleased.*) Ever so many.

CHICHIKOV: Yes, but any particular number?

MANILOV: Yes, exactly what number?

STEWARD: How's a person s'posed to tell the number. Nobody kept any count.

MANILOV: Yes, quite so. (*To* CHICHIKOV.) A very high morality rate; but there's no knowing how many died off.

CHICHIKOV: (*To the* STEWARD.) Please count them up and make a detailed list with their names.

Episode 4

MANILOV: Yes, all of them, with their names.

STEWARD: (*Exiting.*) Yes, sir.

MANILOV: And why do you have to have this?

(*Pause, while* CHICHIKOV *thinks up an answer.*)

CHICHIKOV: Why, you ask? Well, the reasons are: I want to buy some serfs, uh—

MANILOV: Do you want to buy these serfs with land or simply take them with you—without land, I mean?

CHICHIKOV: No, I'm not after peasants exactly. What I'm in the market for is dead ones—

MANILOV: Pardon me . . . I'm a little hard of hearing. I thought you said something peculiar.

CHICHIKOV: I propose to acquire the dead ones, who are still listed with the Census Bureau as being alive.

(MANILOV *drops his pipe in amazement, stares at* CHICHIKOV, *who in return, gets even more dignified.* MANILOV *searches* CHICHIKOV*'s face for signs of insanity.*)

CHICHIKOV: And I'd like to know if you could transfer to me those souls who are not actually alive except legally speaking, in whatever manner suits you best.

(MANILOV *stares, agape.*)

CHICHIKOV: Is there some difficulty about that?

MANILOV: No . . . no, that's not it. But I can't grasp . . . of course, I never enjoyed the brilliant education you display in every move; I'm not adept at self-expression . . . but perhaps . . . in what you have just said . . . there's some hidden meaning . . . you were adopting a metaphoric style?

CHICHIKOV: No, no—I'm talking about really dead souls.

MANILOV: Oh.

CHICHIKOV: Then if there's nothing to stop us, let's make out a deed of sale.

MANILOV: A deed of sale for dead souls?

CHICHIKOV: No, no, we'll put down that they are alive, just as they are entered in the census. I make it a habit never to deviate from the letter of the law even though I've suffered for it in my time; the law stirs up in me a feeling of reverent awe.

MANILOV: Aw—awe

CHICHIKOV: You entertain doubts?

MANILOV: Oh, I wouldn't want you to think that! But permit me to inquire: Won't this enterprise—or if I may use a more all-encompassing expression—this negotiation, won't it be at odds with the ultimate welfare of Russia?

CHICHIKOV: In no way. Moreover, the Treasury will benefit from it, by receiving the registration fee on the deed of sale.

MANILOV: Is it a good thing?

CHICHIKOV: It is a good thing.

MANILOV: Well, in that case, I'm not against it.

CHICHIKOV: All we have to do is agree on a price . . .

MANILOV: A price? How can you imagine I would accept money for souls who are, in a kind of way, passed over into another world? Since you've had such a fantastic, if you don't mind my saying so, whim, I'll let you have them for free.

CHICHIKOV: (*Bursting out of his chair with joy.*) Oh, my heartfelt thanks. There's no way I can express my gratitude . . .

MANILOV: (*Embarrassed.*) It's nothing, I wish there were some way I could really prove my heart's inclination, my soul's magnetism; but as for dead serf souls, they're simply a kind of trash.

CHICHIKOV: They are far from being trash. (*Squeezes* MANILOV*'s hand.*) If you knew the favor you've done me by giving this trash to a man of no lineage or breeding! If you only knew the persecutions I have suffered. Like a bark tossed

Episode 4

on tempestuous waves . . . And what for? For walking the straight and narrow with a clear conscience, extending a helping hand to the bereaved widow and the wretched orphan! (*Dabs away tears.*)

MANILOV: My dear friend. (*Falls into his arms and weeps.* CHICHIKOV *abruptly pulls away and takes his hat.*)

CHICHIKOV: And now I must go!

MANILOV: What, tired of us already! Lizanka, Pavel Ivanovich is leaving!

LIZANKA: (*Entering.*) We must have bored Pavel Ivanovich.

CHICHIKOV: Madam, here, in this very bosom (*Places hand on heart.*) shall dwell the pleasant time I have passed with you! No greater bliss would be for me than to reside, if not in this house, then in close proximity to you.

MANILOV: Oh, if only we could live under the same roof and go in for deep thinking!

CHICHIKOV: (*Sighing.*) Paradise enow! Good-bye, good-bye, madam. Don't forget to come to town with the deed of sale, my friend. Good-bye, my chicks. (*To* THEMISTOCLIUS *and* ALCIDES, *who are quarreling over a toy.*) Excuse me for not bringing you a present, but then I didn't know you existed. Next time, next time. Do you want a sword, Themistoclius?

THEMISTOCLIUS: I wanna.

CHICHIKOV: And how about a drum for you, Alcides?

ALCIDES: (*Shy.*) 'Es, a trum. Boom-boom, boom-boom! (*Once started, he is hard to stop.*)

CHICHIKOV: Goodbye, sweetie. Good-bye!

MANILOV: Do stay, Pavel Ivanovich. Look at those clouds building up!

CHICHIKOV: They're only little clouds. I have to get to Sobakevich's.

SELIFAN: We'll get there, Your Honor. (CHICHIKOV *and* SELIFAN *are off, while the family waves handkerchiefs and stands on tiptoe to watch them depart.*)

MANILOV: (*In a gradual diminuendo.*) Wouldn't it be wonderful to dwell with one's friends on the bank of some river, first building a bridge across the river, then so lofty a belvedere that one could see Moscow from it, and sit there and quaff tea of an evening and discourse on pleasant subjects of some sort; and then the Tsar would come to hear about our profound conversations and our friendship and promote us to the rank of general . . . General Manilov . . . General Chichikov . . . (*He is lost in puffs of smoke.*)

Episode 5

SELIFAN: (*To the horses, giving them a taste of the whip.*) Keep on with your smart tricks and see where that gets you!

CHICHIKOV: Who do you think you're talking to?

SELIFAN: The dapple-gray, the one on the right. He's shirking again.

CHICHIKOV: Oh. (*Settles back with a smile.*)

SELIFAN: Jest you keep yer mind on your work, you German pantaloons, you! You take the sorrel nag, he'll git an extra feedbag o' oats, 'cause he's a horse you can look up to; and Recording Secretary, he's a good horse too. . . . What you twitchin' yer ears fur? Listen, you dummy, when somebody talks to you! I ain't teachin' you nothin' bad, you iggeramus! (*Whip.*) You heathen, you Boneyparte you! You stick to the straight and narrow and folks'll look up to ya! Jest like our boss. He's looked up to ever'wheres he goes, 'cause why? 'Cause he allus done his duty servin' the state, he has—

(*Deafening thunder. Cast members run on stage to create the thunder and lightning by improvised means. Suddenly, amid thunderclaps, a torrential rain pours down.* SELIFAN *shouts to the horses and drives faster.*)

SELIFAN: Hey there, me darlin's! Hey there, me honored friends!

EPISODE 5   25

CHICHIKOV: Selifan!

SELIFAN: Yes, boss.

CHICHIKOV: Look around, is Sobakevich's village in sight?

SELIFAN: No, boss, 'tain't nowheres in sight. . . . Hey there, me certified public accountants! Me fine-feathered functionaries!

CHICHIKOV: You scoundrel, you're off the road! This is a freshly plowed field!

SELIFAN: Well, boss, it's so dark you cain't see the whip afore your face! (*Carriage careens badly.*)

CHICHIKOV: Hold her, hold her, you fool or you'll turn the carriage over!

SELIFAN: No, boss, how could I ever turn it over? That ain't the right thing at all, turning over carriages, I know that my own self; I'd never think o' turnin' it over, no ways. (*The carriage turns over.*) Looky there, if it didn't go and turn over!

CHICHIKOV: You're drunk!

SELIFAN: How could I be drunk! I know it ain't the right thing at all, bein' drunk!

CHICHIKOV: I'll give you a good flogging!

SELIFAN: Just as Yer Honor wishes. If I got to be flogged, then flog me. Flogging's needful, otherwise the peasant gits spilt. If I deserve it, go ahead and flog me—why not?

(*They have been slogging through mud in the dark. A tiny light gleams. They knock at a gate.*)

FETINIYA: (*The housekeeper.*) Who's knocking there? Why are you carrying on like that?

CHICHIKOV: Let us stay the night, old woman!

FETINIYA: What a time to come! This ain't no wayside inn; there's a lady landowner lives here.

CHICHIKOV: We've lost our way. We can't sleep in the open on a night like this.

SELIFAN: It's a dark night and a bad 'un.

CHICHIKOV: Shut up, you idiot.

FETINIYA: And who might you be?

CHICHIKOV: A gentleman, mother.

FETINIYA: A gentleman! Wait a bit, I'll get the mistress.

(*Little by little more and more lamps and candles are lit; while a whole chorus of barking dogs makes itself heard.*)

CHICHIKOV: Judging by that canine chorale, this village must be of considerable size; but I'm too drenched and chilled to think of anything but bed. (*Is led indoors by another servant girl* (GOGOL).)

GOGOL: In a minute, the mistress of the house came in, one of those biddies who are forever complaining about poor crops and at the same time accumulate, bit by bit, tidy little hoards of money, tucked away in various chests of drawers, along with balls of yarns and a cloak with torn seams, destined to be remade into a dress.

CHICHIKOV: I'm very sorry to disturb you, mother.

KOROBOCHKA: Never mind, never mind. What a night for God to send you! Such a nasty storm. . . . You should have a bite to eat, but it's so late I can't have anything cooked for you.

CHICHIKOV: Am I far from town?

KOROBOCHKA: Why, forty mile or thereabouts. I'm so sorry I haven't got anything for you to eat!

CHICHIKOV: Thank you, but a bed will be quite sufficient.

KOROBOCHKA: You just lie down here on this divan, sir. Hey, Fetiniya, fetch a feather bed, some pillows and a sheet! What a night God has sent, what thunder! I've had a candle burning before a holy picture all night long. Heavens to Betsy, kind sir, you're covered in mud like a piggy-wiggy!

CHICHIKOV: Thank God it wasn't worse; it's a blessing I didn't break all my ribs.

EPISODE 5   27

(*During this exchange serf-wenches set up a feather bed, divest* CHICHIKOV *of his outer garments, and brush them carefully. Noise of storm, dogs, etc. continues. Feathers fly from the pillows and mattress.*)

KOROBOCHKA: Land o' Goshen, what you must have gone through! Would you like your back rubbed with something?

CHICHIKOV: No, no thanks, don't go to any trouble!

KOROBOCHKA: There, now, there's your bed all made up. Good-night, kind sir. Is there anything else you'd be needing? Maybe you're used to having a girl scratch your heels at bedtime? My dear departed husband could never fall asleep without that.

CHICHIKOV: (*Has fallen asleep the minute his head hit the pillow; snores.*)

(KOROBOCHKA *and the wenches leave; the sound of snoring, tempest abating, the occasional hissing and whirring of a grandfather clock before it strikes. Sun pours in and the clock strikes ten.*)

GOGOL: As Chichikov awoke and dressed, he looked out the window and fell to contemplating what he beheld: no end of chickens and turkey-hens, with the occasional rooster; a sow bobbed up and while rooting through a dungheap, gobbled up a chick and without noticing it, went on tucking into the watermelon-rinds in a systematic fashion. (*During this description the serf-wenches pick up the feathers, become the poultry, and then do an energetic scrubbing, sweeping, tidying.*) Truck-gardens and fruit orchards stretched into the distance, and the huts of the serfs were well kept and properly looked after.

CHICHIKOV: Not at all a small village, hers.

KOROBOCHKA: How did you sleep, kind sir?

CHICHIKOV: Fine, fine. And yourself, mother?

KOROBOCHKA: Poorly, kind sir.

CHICHIKOV: And what's the cause of your sleeplessness?

KOROBOCHKA: Insomnia. I had a nagging pain in my leg all night long. I rubbed some lard on it and a turpentine compress too. Would you like some fruit brandy with your tea?

CHICHIKOV: I would indeed. (*Sits down at the teatable.*)

KOROBOCHKA: Won't you have a bite? These are mushroom patties, and these are scones, hasty puddings, onion rolls, poppyseed cakes, this is an egg turnover—my kitchen's famous for egg turnovers!

CHICHIKOV: (*Partaking.*) With good reason. Very tasty!

KOROBOCHKA: And won't you have some pancakes?

CHICHIKOV: (*His mouth full of three rolled-up pancakes.*) Delicious!

KOROBOCHKA: Yes, but the crop was poorly; the flour's not what it might be. . . .

CHICHIKOV: But this is a splendid village you've got, mother. How many souls in it?

KOROBOCHKA: Little short of eighty souls, kind sir; but times are hard. God keep us from the poor crops we had last year.

CHICHIKOV: Still, your peasants look to be a sturdy bunch. Sorry, I forgot to ask your name. . . .

KOROBOCHKA: Korobochka, Nastasya Petrovna, widow of a civil servant.

CHICHIKOV: I had an auntie named Nastasya Petrovna. Pretty name.

KOROBOCHKA: And might you be a tax-collector now?

CHICHIKOV: (*Smiling.*) No, heaven forbid, I'm not with the government; just travelling on private business.

KOROBOCHKA: Ah, so you're a purchasing agent! What a pity I sold all my honey to the merchants so cheap, kind sir, for you would have bought it sure.

CHICHIKOV: No, I wouldn't, honey is not at all what I'm after.

KOROBOCHKA: What else, then? Hemp maybe? Dressed or raw?

CHICHIKOV: No, mother, it's a different sort of goods I'm after. Tell me, have any of your peasants died off?

KOROBOCHKA: (*Sighing.*) Oh, kind sir, eighteen of 'em! And all fine workers too. Of course, there's been babies born since then, but what good are they! Babies can't work! And then the tax-collector came along and told me I had to pay tax on the dead ones just like they were alive. Only last week the blacksmith burned up. . . .

CHICHIKOV: You had a fire, mother?

KOROBOCHKA: (*Crossing herself.*) God keep me from such a disaster! No, kind sir, he burned up all on his own; he kept drinking and drinking till a blue flame came out of him, and he smouldered and smouldered till he turned black, like charcoal. What a pity—now there's no one to shoe the horses!

CHICHIKOV: God works in mysterious ways, mother! Let me have them, Nastasya Petrovna!

KOROBOCHKA: Have who?

CHICHIKOV: Why, all the souls that have died off.

KOROBOCHKA: How can I?

CHICHIKOV: Just like that. Or if you like, sell them to me, for cash.

KOROBOCHKA: But how can I? Do you want me to dig them out of the ground?

CHICHIKOV: No, you're way off the mark. It would be a paper transaction merely and the souls will be listed as living.

KOROBOCHKA: (*Eyes popping.*) But whatever do you want them for?

CHICHIKOV: That's my business.

KOROBOCHKA: Yes, but they're dead.

CHICHIKOV: I didn't say they were alive. That's the very reason you take a loss on them: They're dead but you have to keep paying taxes on them. I can rid you of that bother. And I'll give you fifty rubles to boot. Now, is it clear to you?

KOROBOCHKA: (*Hesitating.*) I really don't know. . . . After all, I've never sold any dead souls.

CHICHIKOV: Of course not! It would be a miracle if you had. Or do you think you can use them somehow?

KOROBOCHKA: Oh no! What use could they be? But what troubles me is that they're dead.

CHICHIKOV: (*Aside.*) What a pigheaded hag! (*Aloud.*) Mother dearest, just think, you won't have to pay taxes, and you won't have to bribe officials. I'll take all that on myself. Understand?

KOROBOCHKA: (*Aside.*) It sounds good, but who is he anyway? Maybe he's putting one over on me.

CHICHIKOV: Well, how about it, mother, shall we shake on it?

KOROBOCHKA: Really, kind sir, I've never yet sold dead souls. I did sell some live souls to the parish priest, some three years back—two wenches, a hundred rubles each.

CHICHIKOV: Yes, but we're not talking about live souls, bless them! It's dead ones I'm after.

KOROBOCHKA: I don't know, I'm afraid I'll be taking a loss somehow. They may be worth a lot more. . . .

CHICHIKOV: (*Aside.*) Damn and blast her—her head must be made of solid oak. (*Mops the sweat on his brow with a handkerchief.*) Mother, you refuse to understand me or else you're talking to hear yourself talk . . . I'm giving you fifteen rubles cash, legal tender, got that? Here, here's the money. You won't find that in the gutter. Now, 'fess up, how much did you sell your honey for?

KOROBOCHKA: Ten rubles every thirty pounds.

CHICHIKOV: Never, you never sold it for that. You're sinning with a lie!

EPISODE 5 31

KOROBOCHKA: Swear to God I did!

CHICHIKOV: Well, it fetched that price because it was honey, the fruit of a year's labor. But dead souls are no work of yours, it's God will they passed away. Your labor earned you only ten rubles, but here you get something free, gratis and for nothing, a whole fifteen rubles, and not in silver, but in lovely blue banknotes.

KOROBOCHKA: I'm only a poor widow woman! It might be better if I hold on and see what prices dead souls are fetching nowadays!

CHICHIKOV: This is a disgrace, mother! Stop and think what you're saying! Who would buy them? What could they use them for?

KOROBOCHKA: Well, they might come in handy around the place somehow—

CHICHIKOV: Dead folk around the place! Stick them up in the vegetable patch to scare away crows or what?

KOROBOCHKA: God have mercy on us! What awful things you say! (*Crosses herself.*)

CHICHIKOV: What difference does it make? You keep the bones and the graves; the transfer is on paper. Well, how about it? Give me your answer.

(*Pause.*)

CHICHIKOV: Nastasya Petrovna?

KOROBOCHKA: I think I better sell you the hemp.

CHICHIKOV: Hemp! What's hemp got to do with it! Oh, go to the Devil! (*Bangs a chair on the ground.*)

KOROBOCHKA: (*Crosses herself.*) Oh, don't mention him, God bless him! I dreamt about him all night long. It must have been 'cause I told fortunes at cards after I said my prayers and God sent him as a punishment, with horns longer than my bull's!

CHICHIKOV: I'm surprised horny devils by the dozen don't come to you in your dreams. I'm doing this out of pure

Christian charity. Here I see a poor widow woman working herself to death . . . but now you and your whole village can drop dead for all I care!

KOROBOCHKA: What dreadful curses to wish a body!

CHICHIKOV: As a matter of fact, I was planning to buy up your farm produce because I also supply the government on contracts. . . .

KOROBOCHKA: Why, that's a horse of a different color. Why didn't you say so before? Why get so all-fired angry?

CHICHIKOV: Angry, who's angry? It isn't worth two hoots in hell.

KOROBOCHKA: Well, if you like, I'll gladly let you have them for fifteen rubles. Only listen, about those contracts, if you ever need any flour, or rye or buckwheat. . . . (*As she maunders on and* CHICHIKOV *prepares the papers for signature, the light changes and* GOGOL *steps forward.*)

GOGOL: Why busy ourselves so long with Korobochka? Why not let these things pass us by? For if you stand and contemplate things too long, God knows what odd notions may creep into your head. You may even end up thinking: "Does Korobochka really stand so low on the ladder that leads mankind to perfection? Why, amid carefree moments, does another wondrous strain of thought flash within us? Barely has the laughter faded from our faces, when we have become other persons and our countenances are now illumined with a different. . . .

KOROBOCHKA: Lard! You buying any lard?

CHICHIKOV: (*Packing up and moving to go.*) Why not? Later on, next time.

KOROBOCHKA: And if you need any feathers, I'll have feathers too 'round Christmas time.

CHICHIKOV: Fine, fine. Selifan!

EPISODE 5

SELIFAN: Here, boss.

CHICHIKOV: Now, how do we get back on to the main road?

KOROBOCHKA: Oh dear, there's such a lot of twists and turns. I'll send a little wench with you to show the way. Only, mind you don't carry her off; the merchants have already kidnapped one from me.

CHICHIKOV: (*To* SELIFAN.) What took you so long, you blockhead? Still hung over, I suppose.

KOROBOCHKA: Now, Pelageya, show the gentleman the way.

(CHICHIKOV *gets in the brichka;* PELAGEYA *sits up front with* SELIFAN. *They start off.*)

KOROBOCHKA: Goodbye, kind sir. Keep me in mind when you think of lard! (*To herself.*) I wonder if I missed a trick, selling dead souls for next to nothing, God forbid! Maybe I better go to town and find out what dead souls are fetching. . . .

SELIFAN: Do we turn right now?

PELAGEYA: No, no, I'll show you.

SELIFAN: (*To the horses.*) Giddap, you crow-bait! (*To* PELAGEYA.) Which way now?

PELAGEYA: That way. (*Points.*)

SELIFAN: Oh, you! That *is* the right. You dunno your right from your left! And what's that buildin' over there?

PELAGEYA: That's an inn.

SELIFAN: Well, we'll take it from here by our own selves. You get 'long home. (PELAGEYA *leaps off the carriage.*) You little mud-foot, you!

CHICHIKOV: Here's a kopek for you!

PELAGEYA: (*Runs off chanting.*) I sat on the driver's seat, I sat on the driver's seat. . . .

Episode 6

GOGOL: One of Heaven's greatest gifts to man is a good digestion. Certain pill-popping gentlemen would give half their estates to be able to eat ham at one posting station on the road, sturgeon at another, kielbasa at the next, and then sit down as if they haven't eaten all day and finish up with catfish pie and cabbage dumplings. But our run-of-the-mill hero, Chichikov, had no problems with his appetite.

LANDLADY: (*To* CHICHIKOV *who has got out of the carriage.*) This way, sir!

CHICHIKOV: Have you got a suckling pig?

LANDLADY: That we have.

CHICHIKOV: With horseradish and sour cream?

LANDLADY: With horseradish and sour cream.

CHICHIKOV: Then bring it forth! (*As* LANDLADY *sets table and brings food.*) Do you know the landowner Sobakevich?

LANDLADY: I do indeed, and Squire Manilov as well. That there Manilov is a bit more prefined than Sobakevich; he'll order a chicken and a hunk of veal and if we have any sheep's liver, he'll order sheep's liver, and he'll only take a bite of everything; but Sobakevich'll only order one dish, eat up every bit of it and ask for a extra helping. (*Sound of a carriage driving up.*) At the same price, mind you!

(NOZDRYOV *and* MIZHUEV *enter.*)

NOZDRYOV: (*Flinging his arms wide.*) Ba, ba, ba! What wind blows you this way! (*Embraces and kisses a reluctant* CHICHIKOV; *begins eating out of his dish.*) Look, Mizhuev—you know my brother-in-law, Mizhuev?—Fate has brought us together again! (*To* CHICHIKOV.) Where are you off to now?

CHICHIKOV: Why, I have to see a certain party.

EPISODE 6

NOZDRYOV: Oh, forget him! Let's go to my place!

CHICHIKOV: Impossible, impossible, there's a certain business matter I must attend to.

NOZDRYOV: Business, eh! You're making it up! Oh, you Softsoap Ivanovich!

CHICHIKOV: Honest, it's urgent business.

NOZDRYOV: Ten to one you're lying! Who've you got to see?

CHICHIKOV: Well. . . . Sobakevich.

NOZDRYOV: (*Bursts out laughing.*)

LANDLADY: (*Peering in.*) Something sure must have struck him funny!

NOZDRYOV: Oh, have mercy! I'll bust a gut!

CHICHIKOV: There's nothing funny about it. I gave him my word!

NOZDRYOV: Well, you're barking up the wrong tree if you think you'll get a good game of cards or a bottle of Matradoura from him. Why, that fellow can milk a billy-goat into a sieve! Tell him to go to hell! Let's you and me go to my place! (*Out the window.*) Hey, Porfiry! Bring in that pup! (*To* CHICHIKOV.) It's stolen; its owner would sooner give up his life than that pup. I promised him the chestnut mare—you remember, the one I got from Khvostyryov—

CHICHIKOV: I never heard of any Khvostyryov.

LANDLADY: Would you like a bite of something, sir?

NOZDRYOV: Nothing for me. Ah, brother, what a time we had! On second thought, let me have a glass of vodka.

MIZHUEV: I'll have a glass too, while you're at it.

(LANDLADY *pours out drinks.* PORFIRY *comes in with a puppy.*)

NOZDRYOV: Let me have him. (*Picks him up by the scruff of the neck.*) There's a pup for you! Hey, you didn't comb him out like I told you!

PORFIRY: I did so.

NOZDRYOV: Then why has he got fleas?

PORFIRY: How should I know? Could be they crawled on him from the carriage.

NOZDRYOV: Liar, liar. I think you've given him some of your own. Here, Chichikov (*Tosses puppy to* CHICHIKOV.), look at those ears.

CHICHIKOV: Yes, clearly pedigreed.

NOZDRYOV: And feel how cold his nose is! Touch it!

CHICHIKOV: He has a very keen scent.

NOZDRYOV: I've been hankering after a pug like that for a long time. Porfiry, take him outside! (PORFIRY *takes the puppy out.*) I'm going to feed that puppy on raw meat and turn him into a savage beast. Listen, Chichikov, come to my place right now; it's only three miles or so. After that, you can go to Sobakevich's, if you want.

CHICHIKOV: (*Aside.*) Why not? He's no worse than anyone else, and a bad gambler into the bargain. Perhaps something can be wheedled out of him for free. (*Aloud.*) Let's go then; but don't detain me. My time is precious.

MIZHUEV: Let me out of it. I have to be getting home.

NOZDRYOV: Nonsense, nonsense, don't think of it! (*They get up to go.*)

LANDLADY: You haven't paid for the vodka yet, sir.

NOZDRYOV: Ah, right you are! Say, brother-in-law, cover me, will you? I haven't a penny on me!

MIZHUEV: How much is it?

LANDLADY: Twenty kopeks in all, kind sir.

NOZDRYOV: Liar, liar! Give her half, that's more than enough.

(*They set off:* NOZDRYOV, MIZHUEV *and* CHICHIKOV *in* CHICHIKOV*'s brichka and* MIZHUEV*'s carriage side-by-side;* PORFIRY *and the puppy trailing behind in* NOZDRYOV*'s calash.*)

EPISODE 6

GOGOL: Nozdryov was one of those hail-fellows-well-met who can sniff out a ball or a party at twenty miles distance and be there in a twinkling, argufying and stirring up a rumpus at the card-tables. Since he was up to sundry tricks, the game would often culminate in another sort of game: kicking and drubbing and mangling of side-whiskers. But—and this can only happen in Russia—after a while he would meet the friends who had thrashed him and they'd act as if nothing had ever happened.

NOZDRYOV: Look at that roan stallion, I paid ten thousand for him.

MIZHUEV: You never! He isn't worth a thousand!

NOZDRYOV: By God, I did so give ten thousand.

MIZHUEV: Swear till you're blue in the face.

NOZDRYOV: Want to make a bet?

GOGOL: To some degree, Nozdryov was a man of affairs. Wherever he was, an affair would crop up: He'd get so looped at the drinks table that all he could do was laugh. Or else lie such a blue streak, that his audience would run for their lives.

NOZDRYOV: In that field over there, there's such an awful lot of rabbits you can't see the ground for them. I caught one by the hindlegs with my hands.

MIZHUEV: You can't catch a rabbit with your bare hands.

NOZDRYOV: Well I did.

GOGOL: And Nozdryov had a passion for playing low-down tricks for no earthly reason. The more intimate he became with anybody, the more willingly would he put the skids under him, spreading tall tales, breaking up marriages or business deals, and never ceasing to consider him his dearest friend.

NOZDRYOV: (*To* CHICHIKOV.) Now I'll take you to the boundary line where my land ends—everything you see on this side is mine and that blue forest is mine and everything beyond the forest—that's mine too.

MIZHUEV: Since when did that forest become yours? It wasn't yours before.

(*They emerge from the carriage to* NOZDRYOV's *house. During* GOGOL's *next speech,* NOZDRYOV *changes into a dressing gown, and they begin to drink.*)

NOZDRYOV: I bought it recently.

MIZHUEV: How did you manage to buy it so quickly?

NOZDRYOV: I bought it three days ago, and for a devilish high price too.

MIZHUEV: But you were at the fair then—

NOZDRYOV: Oh, you bumpkin! I was at the fair, but my steward bought it while I was away.

MIZHUEV: Well, the Steward might've.

GOGOL: Food was not a prime consideration in life for Nozdryov; his chef was guided by inspiration and would pop into the pot whatever came to hand: pepper, milk, peas, ham—slap dash, so long it was hot, and as to taste, well, some sort of taste would emerge. Nozdryov put his faith in wine.

NOZDRYOV: (*Pouring out glass after glass as he circles the table.*) This is port, and here's a Haut Sauterne, no ordinary sauternes around here. Now this Madeira is such that even the field marshal has never drunk a better. This one's a bourginion and a champignion rolled into one. And this cordial tastes exactly like cream.

(CHICHIKOV *and* MIZHUEV *have glasses in each hand.* MIZHUEV *downs his as soon as they're filled, but* CHICHIKOV *tries pouring his into* NOZDRYOV's *and* MIZHUEV's *empty glasses.*)

MIZHUEV: (*Dead drunk.*) I've really got to be going!

NOZDRYOV: Never, never, I won't let you. We'll get up a little game of cards.

MIZHUEV: No, brother, you're planning to take 'vantish of me. My wife's gonna be in high dungeon. Don't hold me back.

NOZDRYOV: Oh, to hell with you and your wife. Somebody'd think the two of you were going to do something important together.

MIZHUEV: No, brother, she's za sweetes' li'l wife in the worl'—! The things she does for me—makes the tears come to my eyes. I'm going! Cross my heart—

CHICHIKOV: (*Undertone.*) Let him go. What good is he?

NOZDRYOV: True enough. I hate people who can't hold their liquor. Oh, go crochet doilies with your wife, you tame twat!

MIZHUEV: Don't call me a tame twat, brother. She's za sweetes' li'l wife in the worl', breaks my heart.

NOZDRYOV: Go on, tell her lies. Here's your cap.

MIZHUEV: Forgive me for not staying, I'd love to, but I can't. I got to tell my wife all about the fair.

NOZDRYOV: Porfiry!

(PORFIRY *enters, shoulders the still-protecting* MIZHUEV, *and carries him out.*)

NOZDRYOV: A horse's ass, pure and simple. (*Pulls out a pack of cards and does fancy shuffles.*) Well, what do you say, brother? Shall we start at three hundred, just to pass the time?

CHICHIKOV: Ah! Before it slips my mind, I have a certain request to make you.

NOZDRYOV: What is it?

CHICHIKOV: First, give me your word you'll grant it.

NOZDRYOV: But what is it?

CHICHIKOV: Your word of honor!

NOZDRYOV: My word of honor!

CHICHIKOV: All right. I suppose you have a large number of dead serfs who haven't been removed from the tax rolls yet. Transfer them to me in my name.

NOZDRYOV: What for?

CHICHIKOV: I happen to need them.

NOZDRYOV: But what for?

CHICHIKOV: I just happen to need them . . . for reasons of my own.

NOZDRYOV: You've got something cooking for sure. Own up—what is it?

CHICHIKOV: What difference does it make to you? It's just a whim of mine.

NOZDRYOV: Well, until you tell me, I won't go through with it.

CHICHIKOV: (*After reflection.*) You see, I need these dead serfs to acquire a position in society, especially since I don't own any large estates.

NOZDRYOV: Liar, liar! You're a liar, brother!

CHICHIKOV: Very well, I'll lay my cards on the table, but please don't tell anyone. I've decided to marry but my in-laws-to-be are ambitious and want the bridegroom to have no fewer than three hundred souls, and I only have one hundred and fifty—

NOZDRYOV: Liar, liar!

CHICHIKOV: I haven't lied even that much. (*Shows tip of his finger.*)

NOZDRYOV: I'll stake my head you're lying!

CHICHIKOV: How insulting! Why am I supposed to be lying?

NOZDRYOV: Oh, I know you, you're a swindler de luxe, if an old friend may say so! If I were your boss, I'd hang you from the first tree that came along!

CHICHIKOV: (*Genuinely offended.*) This is the limit. If you wish to make speeches like that, I suggest to go to a barracks. If you won't give them to me, sell them.

NOZDRYOV: Sell them! You bastard! What sort of price would you give for them?

CHICHIKOV: What, are your souls made of diamonds or something?

NOZDRYOV: Tell you what, just to prove I'm not stingy, I won't take anything for the souls. Buy my stallion off me and I'll throw the souls in.

CHICHIKOV: What would I do with a stallion, I don't run a stud-farm!

NOZDRYOV: Or look, buy this hurdy-gurdy from me. This is what I call an organ! Solid mahogany! (*He plays it; the tune is "For He's a Jolly Good Fellow."*) I'll throw it away for nine hundred.

CHICHIKOV: What would I be doing with a hurdy-gurdy? I'm no Italian to lug it up and down, begging for pennies.

NOZDRYOV: Then we'll swap: the hurdy-gurdy *and* the dead souls for your carriage and three hundred rubles.

CHICHIKOV: Don't want it—and that's all there is to it.

NOZDRYOV: You're a real so-and-so! Tell you what, let's have a little game of cards. I'll stake all the dead souls on one card, and the hurdy-gurdy too. (*Starts shuffling cards.*)

CHICHIKOV: Deciding by cards means leaving it all to chance.

NOZDRYOV: What's chancy about it? It's luck, and luck's your middle name!

CHICHIKOV: To tell the truth, I don't care for playing cards.

NOZDRYOV: And why don't you?

CHICHIKOV: (*Shrugging.*) Because I don't.

NOZDRYOV: You pile of garbage!

CHICHIKOV: What can I do? That's how God made me.

NOZDRYOV: You tame twat! I was going to let you have those souls for nothing, but now I wouldn't give them to you for three kingdoms. You shill, you chimneysweep! (*Shouts out window.*) Porfiry, tell them in the stables not to give his horses any oats—let 'em eat hay. (*To* CHICHIKOV.) Never darken my door again! (CHICHIKOV *starts to leave. Suddenly:*) How about a game of checkers? If you win, they're all yours.

CHICHIKOV: Don't put yourself out—I won't play.

NOZDRYOV: This isn't like cards, there's no luck or trickery here—it all depends on skill. (*Arranges checkers on board.*)

CHICHIKOV: (*Aside.*) What can I lose? I used to be good at checkers and it would be hard to pull any tricks in this game. (*Aloud.*) So be it! Make it a game of checkers.

NOZDRYOV: How many checkers will you give me as a handicap?

CHICHIKOV: Why should I?

NOZDRYOV: Then let me have two extra moves, at least.

CHICHIKOV: I will not. I'm a poor player myself.

NOZDRYOV: We know all about you so-called poor players. (*Moves a checker.*)

CHICHIKOV: It's been ages since I played. (*Moves a checker.*)

NOZDRYOV: We know all about you alleged poor players. (*Moves a checker.*)

CHICHIKOV: It's been ages since I played. (*Moves a checker.*)

NOZDRYOV: We know all about you putative poor players. (*Moves three checkers using the sleeve of his dressing-gown.*)

CHICHIKOV: It's been ages since—hey, what's all that? You move that one back!

NOZDRYOV: Move what back?

CHICHIKOV: That checker, the one that's heading for king's row. Where the hell did that come from? (*Rising.*) No, it's absolutely impossible to play with you. People aren't supposed to move three checkers at a time!

NOZDRYOV: It was a mistake, it moved forward by accident. I'll move it back, if you like.

CHICHIKOV: And the other one? That's the square where it belongs!

NOZDRYOV: What square? You're making things up!

CHICHIKOV: No, brother, you're the one making things up—and pretty clumsily at that.

NOZDRYOV: Are you calling me a cheat?

CHICHIKOV: I'm not calling you anything, I just won't play with you any more.

NOZDRYOV: You can't quit now that the game's started!

CHICHIKOV: I can, because you're not playing like an honest man!

NOZDRYOV: Liar, liar!

CHICHIKOV: Liar yourself! Try and make me finish the game. (*Messes up all the checkers.*)

NOZDRYOV: (*Flares up, walking so close to* CHICHIKOV *he forces him to retreat.*) Oh no you don't. I remember all the moves. I'll put them back the way they were.

CHICHIKOV: No, it's finished; I'm not going to play with you.

NOZDRYOV: Why don't you come right out and say you don't want to play? (*Marching on him.*)

CHICHIKOV: I don't want to . . . (NOZDRYOV *takes a swing at him but* CHICHIKOV *holds him fast by the wrists.*)

NOZDRYOV: Porfiry! Porfiry! (*Wriggling to get free.*)

(CHICHIKOV *releases* NOZDRYOV*'s hands.*)

NOZDRYOV: So when you see you aren't winning, you refuse to play? (PORFIRY *enters.*) Beat him up! Beat him up! Beat him up!

(NOZDRYOV, *yelling, sweating, clutching his chibouk like a club, strains forward;* CHICHIKOV, *ashen, his lips moving feverishly, grabs a chair to defend himself;* PORFIRY *lumbers toward him and wrests the chair away.*)

GOGOL: Freeze! (*They do so.* GOGOL *considers the tableau for a minute, as if devising a way out. He snaps his fingers and* NOZDRYOV *and* PORFIRY *knock down* CHICHIKOV.) No, don't like that. (*Snaps his fingers.* CHICHIKOV *karate-chops* NOZDRYOV *and* PORFIRY, *who fall.*) No, don't like that. (*Then, he dons a moustache, a military frock-coat and a police cap.*) Which one of you is Nozdryov?

NOZDRYOV: Whom have I the honor of addressing?

GOGOL: I am Captain of the Rural Police.

NOZDRYOV: What do you want?

GOGOL: I must inform you that you are under arrest until such time as a final verdict is handed down in your case.

NOZDRYOV: What crap! What case?

GOGOL: You are implicated in a lawsuit involving a personal assault, with birch rods, on the person of one Maksimov, a landowner, while under the influence of alcohol.

NOZDRYOV: Liar, liar! I never set eyes on any Maksimov!

GOGOL: Sir! Let me inform you that I am an officer of the law. You can talk that way to your servant but not to me!

(*Meanwhile,* CHICHIKOV *has made a stealthy escape, slipped into his carriage, and woken* SELIFAN.)

CHICHIKOV: Selifan! Selifan! Whip up the horses and drive for all they're worth!

Episode 7

(*The carriage careens along at breakneck speed.* CHICHIKOV *pants with fright and pats his heart.*)

CHICHIKOV: (*Breathless.*) What a fine kettle of fish that was! Lucky thing that Police Captain showed up when he did, or

I would have sunk without a trace, with no posterity, and no property or honorable name to bequeath to them!

SELIFAN: Nasty sort o'host he was! Makes you want to spit, know what I mean? Don't matter what you feed a man, but you gotta give his horse oats. Them's a horse's nat'ral vittles.

(*Suddenly the brichka crashes into a barouche containing a* YOUNG LADY [*the* GOVERNOR'S DAUGHTER] *and an* OLD LADY.)

BAROUCHE COACHMAN: You chiseler you! I was yelling, "Take a right, you crow!" You drunk or what?

SELIFAN: And where do you get off, travellin' at a speed like that? You pawn your eyes at a tavern or something?

BAROUCHE COACHMAN: Back 'er up, you small-time crow!

(*They attempt a series of maneuvers to untangle the harness, but every time they back up the horses step over the traces and collide again. A knot of peasants gathers; some of them undo the traces and part the horses, but despite whipping, certain horses won't budge.*)

PEASANTS: (*Ad lib.*) Go on, Andryushka, you lead away the horse on the right side. Uncle Mityay, git up on the shaft-horse! Git up there, Uncle Mityay!

(UNCLE MITYAY, *spare, lanky, red-bearded, perches on one horse, but to no avail.*)

PEASANTS: Hold on, hold on! Now, Uncle Mityay, you git up on the t'other horse, and let Uncle Minyay git up on the shaft-horse.

(UNCLE MITYAY, *black-bearded, big-bellied, broad-shouldered, gets on the shaft-horse, which collapses to the ground beneath him.*)

PEASANTS: Now we're gittin' somewheres! Make it hot for him! Give 'im a taste of the whip! What's he buckin' fer, like a coramora?

GOGOL: A coramora is a long, torpid mosquito which can be grasped by the leg and will react by arching himself, or bucking, as the common people put it.

(*More maneuvers:* UNCLE MITYAY *and* UNCLE MINYAY *both get on the shaft-horse, until the* BAROUCHE COACHMAN *chases them away.* CHICHIKOV *meanwhile goes to the* LADIES *and tries to start a conversation.*)

CHICHIKOV: How 'do, ladies! I'm extremely distressed by this awkward contretemps . . . uh. . . . These are the accidents of the road . . . that . . . travellers encounter when . . . uh . . . (*Because the* OLD LADY *is palpitating and the* YOUNG LADY *is on the verge of tears, the conversation does not take fire.*)

BAROUCHE COACHMAN: We're all set now, ma'am.

OLD LADY: Drive on!

(*The barouche and its occupants drive away. The peasants, after more ad lib commentary, disperse.*)

GOGOL: Wherever his life may run its course, amid the squalidly mildewing lower classes, or the monotonously frigid upper classes, once at least man is fated to encounter a phenomenon unlike anything else he has ever experienced. Running counter to the sorrows that fill our life, a glittering joy will gaily flash by, like a golden coach speeding through a dreary backwoods hamlet. In such a way did this sixteen-year-old blonde suddenly appear in our story and disappear in the same way. If, instead of Chichikov, some youth of twenty had happened to be here—the things that would have awakened, stirred and found a voice within him! As it is. . . .

CHICHIKOV: (*Taking snuff.*) Pretty bit of fluff! Just come out of finishing school, most likely. Now she's a mere child, who'll say whatever comes into her mind. She can be made into a miracle or she may turn out so much trash—and will! Let the mamas and aunties get their hands on here and in a year she'll be pumped so full of ladylikeness her own father won't recognize her. The Devil's own mess! Though if she gets a dowry of, say, two hundred thousand, she might make some decent fellow happy. Hmmm. Maybe I should have asked her name. (*He has got into the carriage and is riding again.*)

Episode 7

GOGOL: On *his* estate, Sobakevich had taken great pains to achieve solidity—everything was constructed of stout timbers meant to last for decades. As Chichikov drove up, he noticed a face in the window—round and broad, like those pumpkins (*A pumpkin is flung forward.*) which Russians make into two-stringed light balalaikas, the pride and joy of some merrry country lad, a dandy who winks and whistles (*The pumpkin has become a balalaika in the hands of a youth.*) at the snowy-breasted, snowy-necked maidens who listen to his soft strumming. (*The pumpkin becomes the head of* SOBAKEVICH. *The music stops.*)

SOBAKEVICH: Come on in. (*Introducing his wife, a tall, bony woman.*) This is my Feoduliya Ivanovna.

(CHICHIKOV *advances to kiss her hand, which she shoves into his mouth.*)

CHICHIKOV: The lady's been making dill pickles, I perceive!

SOBAKEVICH: My pet, this is Pavel Ivanovich Chichikov! Let's go to dinner!

(*A gargantuan repast is laid out.* SOBAKEVICH *eats huge quantities of everything.*)

SOBAKEVICH: The cabbage soup is awfully good today, m'dear. (*To* CHICHIKOV.) You won't find a pudding like that in town!

CHICHIKOV: What's in it?

SOBAKEVICH: It's a ram's stomach, stuffed with buckwheat, brains, and sheep's feet! Real eating! And how let's adjourn to the drawing-room.

CHICHIKOV: (*Aside, rising.*) I feel thirty-five pounds heavier!

MRS SOBAKEVICH: Have some dessert. Radish stewed in honey!

SOBAKEVICH: We'll tackle it later. Go to your room. Pavel Ivanovich and I'll have a bit of a rest. (*She exits. They sit in easy chairs.*)

CHICHIKOV: There's a certain little matter I'd like to discuss with you. (SOBAKEVICH *cocks his head in a listening posture.*) The realm of Russia is so extensive even ancient Rome was not so great, and foreigners are right to be astonished . . . hmmm . . . uh, also, owing to present conditions in this glorious realm, serfs listed in the census, though they may have departed this earthly vale, are nonetheless considered by the Tax Office as alive, until the new census, so as not to complicate an already complex governmental machinery . . . uh, uh . . . so notwithstanding the justice of the law, on occasion it proves burdensome to serf-owners, forcing them to pay taxes on souls regarded as living chattels though actually dea—uh, nonexistent, and I, out of personal regard for you, am ready to assume this onerous obligation. (SOBAKEVICH *hasn't twitched.*)

SOBAKEVICH: You need dead souls?

CHICHIKOV: Yes. That is, nonexistent souls.

SOBAKEVICH: They can be found.

CHICHIKOV: And you would be glad to get rid of them?

SOBAKEVICH: For a price, yes.

CHICHIKOV: (*Aside.*) Damn it, this fellow is already selling them! (*Aloud.*) And what price would you be asking, for instance? Although . . . it seems silly to talk about prices.

SOBAKEVICH: Well, not to go too high, a hundred rubles a head!

CHICHIKOV: A hundred rub . . .

SOBAKEVICH: Why, is that too expensive? What's your price then?

CHICHIKOV: My price! There's clearly a misunderstanding here. We're forgetting what's at issue. With hand on heart, I protest my top price is eighty kopeks a soul. I can't in all conscience give more than that.

SOBAKEVICH: I'm not selling bark sandals.

CHICHIKOV: All the same, they aren't what you'd call people.

SOBAKEVICH: So you think you'll find a fool dumb enough to sell you a soul listed in the Census for a couple of kopeks?

CHICHIKOV: Why do you describe them that way? They've died long ago; nothing is left of them but an insubstantial word. However, to make a long story short, I'll give you a ruble and a half. My final offer.

SOBAKEVICH: You should be ashamed. If you want to do business, name a real price.

CHICHIKOV: I can't, I absolutely can't. I'll tack on another half a ruble.

SOBAKEVICH: What are you so stingy for? Some swindler will hoodwink you and sell you trash, not souls; whereas mine are all hale and hearty, hand-picked. Mikheyev, for instance, a coachmaker! Why every vehicle he turned out seemed to run on springs. And solid! And he'd upholster and varnish it himself!

CHICHIKOV: But . . .

SOBAKEVICH: And Corky Stepan the carpenter? The strength in him! Seven foot one and three quarter inches tall he was!

CHICHIKOV: Don't you see that . . .

SOBAKEVICH: And Milushkin the bricklayer.

CHICHIKOV: You don't seem to under . . .

SOBAKEVICH: And Maksim Telyatnikov the shoemaker: he'd run his hand over a piece of leather and there'd be a pair of boots. And never touched a drop! That's the kind of people they are!

CHICHIKOV: But, excuse me, why enumerate all their good points? They're all dead. All a dead body's good for is propping up a fence.

SOBAKEVICH: Of course they're dead. And you call the people living nowadays alive? They're insects, not people.

CHICHIKOV: You're an intelligent, well-educated man. I don't understand why you're staging this act. Why, what can such stuff be worth? Who needs it?

SOBAKEVICH: You do, since you want to buy it.

CHICHIKOV: (*After a pause.*) Two rubles apiece. My last word.

SOBAKEVICH: And my last word is fifty rubles a head. I'm taking a loss: Try and get good serfs cheaper anywhere!

CHICHIKOV: (*Vexed.*) Why, anybody else would give them to me for free, to be rid of them. Only a fool would want to pay taxes on them!

SOBAKEVICH: But don't you know that purchases of this sort—this is strictly between ourselves, as friends—aren't exactly condoned, and if word got out, the buyer of such souls would be in a lot of trouble.

CHICHIKOV: (*With feigned disconcern.*) As you like. If you won't take two and a half, I'll bid you good-day.

SOBAKEVICH: Well, go with God, make it thirty rubles a head and they're yours!

CHICHIKOV: No, I see you don't want to sell. (*Makes to go.*)

SOBAKEVICH: (*Stepping on his foot.*) Hold on, hold on!

CHICHIKOV: Owww!

SOBAKEVICH: (*Thrusting him into an armchair.*) Sorry to inconvenience you.

CHICHIKOV: I'm in a hurry.

SOBAKEVICH: Just a minute, I'll tell you something you'll like. (*In a whisper.*) You want to clinch the bargain?

CHICHIKOV: My last price is two and a half.

SOBAKEVICH: You rate a soul the same as a boiled turnip! Make it three rubles, at least.

CHICHIKOV: I can't.

SOBAKEVICH: What can I do with you, take them if you like. I'm suffering a loss, but I guess I'm just a puppy-dog at heart. I suppose we'll have to go to town to execute the purchase-deed?

EPISODE 7

CHICHIKOV: Of course.

SOBAKEVICH: I'll make out a list. (*While* SOBAKEVICH *composes his list,* CHICHIKOV *rhapsodizes.*)

CHICHIKOV: (*Aside*) Were you born the bear you are or were you turned into a bear by your backwoods life? No, you'd be the same if you lived in the city. Now you rule over peasants and you deal fairly with them, since you own them and it would do you no good to abuse them; in the city, you'd be in charge of a lot of crooks or you'd be dipping your fingers in the Public till. Oh, I wish all these tight-fisted characters would go to—

SELIFAN: Women? Want any female souls? Cheap, a ruble a head.

CHICHIKOV: No, thank you. I can't use females. They have no legal standing.

SOBAKEVICH: Oh well, one man's maid is another man's person. Here's the list then.

CHICHIKOV: Why, it's a delight—so meticulous and accurate.

SOBAKEVICH: And now a small deposit, if you plese.

CHICHIKOV: Why? You'll be paid in full in town.

SOBAKEVICH: It's the usual thing.

CHICHIKOV: I don't know. I didn't bring any money with me. Oh, yes, here are ten rubles.

SOBAKEVICH: Be serious. Fifty rubles at least.

CHICHIKOV: I don't have that much money on me.

SOBAKEVICH: Yes you do.

CHICHIKOV: Well, here's fifteen more, that makes twenty-five. But please give me a receipt.

SOBAKEVICH: What do you need a receipt for?

CHICHIKOV: It's the usual thing.

SOBAKEVICH: All right, hand over the money.

CHICHIKOV: Why? You can get it as soon as you hand over the receipt.

SOBAKEVICH: Very well. (*He writes a receipt. They execute a gingerly exchange,* CHICHIKOV *releasing the banknotes only when* SOBAKEVICH *releases the receipt.*) This note is torn; but friends shouldn't be too fussy

CHICHIKOV: (*Aside.*) Goddamned tightwad! And a bastard to boot. (*Aloud.*) There's one other thing: This deal should remain in the strictest confidence.

SOBAKEVICH: That goes without saying. Thanks for the visit. Lucky for you you did business with *me*. Someone else would have driven you a hard bargain. Plyushkin, for instance. Owns eight hundred souls and lives worse than a convict.

CHICHIKOV: Who's this Plyushkin?

SOBAKEVICH: A swindler, a miser to end all misers. He's starved all his serfs to death.

CHICHIKOV: Really? His people are dying in great numbers?

SOBAKEVICH: Like flies.

CHICHIKOV: How dreadful. Where does he live?

SOBAKEVICH: (*Takes a long look at* CHICHIKOV *and bursts out laughing.*)

Episode 8

(*Under* SOBAKEVICH'S *watchful eye,* CHICHIKOV *has jumped in the brichka and ridden off.*)

CHICHIKOV: (*To a* PEASANT TOTING A LOG ON HIS SHOULDERS.) Hey, you there, you with the beard! How does one get from here to Plyushkin's place? (*Long pause of hesitation.*) Well, don't you know?

EPISODE 8

PEASANT WITH LOG: No, boss, I don't.

CHICHIKOV: And your hair's gone gray! Plyushkin! Haven't you ever heard of Plyushkin, the miser, the fellow who feeds his people so badly?

PEASANT WITH LOG: Oh, the raggedy mother (*mouths "-fucker", but a censoring bleep covers his words.*), the raggedy mother (*-f, bleep.*).

GOGOL: What a powerful way the Russian people have of expressing themselves! If they bestow an apt epithet on any man, it will descend to his posterity and he'll drag it along with him to the ends of the earth. Russian wit comes straight out with a word and doesn't brood over it like a setting hen; a man is delineated at a stroke, from head to foot. There is nothing in this world that can be so sweeping, so boisterous, so eruptive, so heartfelt, so seething and quivering and fluttering like a living thing, as an aptly uttered Russian word!

PEASANT WITH LOG: Ah, the raggedy mother-(*BLEEP!*) (*The lighting grows more somber.*)

GOGOL: As Chichikov mulled over the nickname the peasants had given Plyushkin, he failed to notice that he had driven into the center of an extensive settlement, the huts tumbled-down and full of holes. The walls of the manor house showed cracks and blotches and most of the windows were shuttered or boarded over. The old, immense garden had gone to seed, choked with weeds and overgrown, but it was the only thing to give an air of freshness to the picture of desolation. Chichikov soon noticed a figure bickering with a peasant, but for a long while he could not determine the sex of the figure.

CHICHIKOV: (*To himself.*) It's a peasant woman. . . . No, the voice is too hoarse. . . . Of course, it's a woman. Must be the housekeeper. (*Aloud, getting out of the carriage.*) Say, mother, is your master—

PLYUSHKIN: Ain't to home. (*Pause.*) What you want with him?

CHICHIKOV: I'm here on business.

PLYUSHKIN: Git in the house!

GOGOL: (*Like mirror images, back to back,* GOGOL *and* CHICHIKOV *slowly explore the spaces, coming together and revolving under the chandelier.*) Chichikov stepped into a dark wide entry that blew cold at him as from a cellar, and then into a room dimly lit by a single candle. There was a general disorder, as of spring housecleaning, with furniture piled up from time immemorial: a clock with its pendulum stopped, a bureau whose mother-of-pearl mosaic was chipped and fragmented; mounds of paper, a marble paperweight turned green, a lemon dried to the size of a walnut, and a toothpick whose owner must have been picking his teeth with it even before Napoleon entered Moscow. From the middle of the ceiling hung a chandelier in a canvas bag, so covered in dust it looked like a silk cocoon with the larva inside.

CHICHIKOV: Well, what about your master? Is he at home or not?

PLYUSHKIN: You blind or something? I'm the master!

CHICHIKOV: (*Aside.*) Good Lord, if I'd run into him outside a church, I'd have slipped him a penny.

GOGOL: This was no beggar, but a landowner possessing a thousand serfs and a plenitude of wheat, linens, cloth, sheepskins dressed and raw, dried fish, vegetables and salt meat, every sort of wood and utensil, and a host of wares. Even so, Plyushkin would patrol his grounds, peering under bridges and planks, to snap up everything he came upon— shoe soles, a rag, a nail, a broken pot—and add it to the pile in the room. And yet there was a time when he was only an economical householder! (*The lighting changes to a theatrical gaslit glare. The following account is pantomimed in the style of Victorian melodrama. Atmospheric music is played under this scene.*) The master was bustling and intelligent, his wife affable and talkative, his pretty daughter was fresh as a rose, his son a sprightly little ragamuffin, and the governess fair and French. But the good lady of the house died; her keys and her cares passed to Plyushkin, who, like most widowers, became more suspicious and niggardly. His elder daughter

Episode 8

ran off with a cavalry captain and married him hurriedly in a village church, for her father had no love for military men, thinking them gamblers and scalawags. His wedding present was a curse. Madame La Gouvernante was packed off for having had a hand in the affair. The son was sent to the county seat to go into the civil service; he joined a regiment instead and when he wrote home for money, the answer he got was what the peasants call "Up yours!" The old man was left sole watchman and guardian of his wealth. Every year more windows were boarded up and the master became more withdrawn; his hay and wheat rotted and his cloth turned to dust; yet every year his revenue and wares kept accumulating, for the peasants were still obliged to bring in their allotment of produce and linen and rent. (*A stream of peasants dumps more stuff in the room and they themselves become furniture and detritus.*) All these goods were dumped into storerooms to rot, and Plyushkin himself turned at last into a rip in the cloak of humanity. (*The stage is totally cluttered.*)

CHICHIKOV: (*Recovering from his surprise.*) Uh, my dear sir, having heard of your economy and rare skill in managing estates, I deemed it my duty to pay you my respects in person.

PLYUSHKIN: (*Mumbling.*) To hell with you, respects and all. (*Louder.*) Please take a seat. It's a coon's age since I seen any callers and I can live without 'em. You got to give their horses hay! There ain't so much as a wisp o' hay in the place! And there ain't no peasants to work this miserable piece of land—they're always sneaking off to the tavern . . . chances are, I'll end up in the poorhouse in my old age!

CHICHIKOV: (*Discreetly.*) Still, I've been told you own over a thousand souls.

PLYUSHKIN: And who went and told you that? You should of spit in his eye! A thousand souls! Just you go and count 'em and see what it comes to. These last three years that damned fever's been and carried off a good passel of my peasants.

CHICHIKOV: Is that so? Many have been carried off?

PLYUSHKIN: Plenty.

CHICHIKOV: Exactly how many?

PLYUSHKIN: Eighty head.

CHICHIKOV: No!

PLYUSHKIN: Why should I lie about it? Fact is, it's a good hundred and twenty souls since the last census.

CHICHIKOV: (*Joyously.*) A whole hundred and twenty.

PLYUSHKIN: There's no call for you to git so happy.

CHICHIKOV: Not to beat around the bush, I'm prepared to assume the obligation of paying taxes on all those serfs who have died since the last census.

PLYUSHKIN: (*After a pause of stupefaction.*) But don't that mean you'd be losing money?

CHICHIKOV: To please you, I'd be glad to lose money.

PLYUSHKIN: (*Snuff dripping from his nose, his dressing gown slipping open in his ecstasy.*) Ah, my benefactor! My father! Oh Lord! Oh saints in heaven! (*Mops his face with his crumpled handkerchief.*) Now how are you goin' to do it? Do you pay me the money or does the Treasury?

CHICHIKOV: This is how we'll work it. We'll put through a deed of sale as if they were still alive and you had sold them to me.

PLYUSHKIN: (*Gnawing his lips.*) Ah, yes, a deed o' sale. Now that there means expenses. And you know well as me what clerks is like these days. Used to be you could slip 'em half a ruble and a bag o' flour, now they're so hoity-toity, you got to give 'em a whole wagonload o' grits and a ten-ruble note! I dunno why the priests don't make a sermon on it. . . . Say what you like, nothin' can withstand the Word of God.

CHICHIKOV: (*Aside.*) You could. (*Aloud.*) I shall take that expense on myself, dear friend.

PLYUSHKIN: (*Overjoyed.*) You would! (*Walks over to window.*) Hey, Proshka! (*To* CHICHIKOV.) You ain't in the military, I hope?

EPISODE 8   57

CHICHIKOV: No, I was in the Civil Service.

(PROSHKA *a barefoot boy of thirteen, enters and puts on enormous boots at the threshold, before proceeding into the room.*)

PLYUSHKIN: Look at that kisser, would ya! Why he's as thick as a stump, but just you leave anything lying around, he'll steal it in a twinkling! (*To* PROSHKA.) Here, dummy, take this key, give it to Mavra and have her go to the storeroom; on a shelf there's a Easter cake my daughter sent me last year . . . have it served up! Hold on, where're you off to? You big booby! You got ants in your pants? Listen, the frosting's probably mouldy, so have her scrape over the top with a knife, but don't throw the crumbs away—take 'em to feed the chickens. And don't you set foot in that storeroom yourself! I'll be watchin' ya from this window!

(PROSHKA *takes off the boots and leaves.* PLYUSHKIN *rummages through a dresser which he opens with a key on his keyring.*)

PLYUSHKIN: There, can't find it. I had a tasty little cordial, but my people is such thieves! Ah, here it is! (*Blows a heavy layer of dust off the bottle.*) My late wife made it herself. Just let me fish these bugs out and I'll pour you a glass.

CHICHIKOV: No thank you, I've already dined and wined.

PLYUSHKIN: Already wined and dined! You can tell a man who moves in good society, he eats and drinks before he comes! Oh, but you'll need a list of all my loafers! (*Starts rummaging through papers, after putting on his spectacles.*) Here we are. (*Comes upon a paper, crammed with miniscule writing, filling every blank space.*)

CHICHIKOV: (*Reading it.*) More than a hundred and twenty! Many thanks. (*Pockets the document.*) Of course you'll have to come to town to formalize the deed of sale.

PLYUSHKIN: To town? How can I? How can I leave the house? This pack of sneak-thieves'll strip me bare, rob me blind.

CHICHIKOV: Haven't you some friend in town who can act as your proxy?

PLYUSHKIN: What friend? All my friends is either dead or ain't friends no more. . . . There must be somebody . . . Of course! Why, I know the Bureau Chief himself. (*A ray of warmth illumines his face.*) We used to climb fences together! Of course, we're friends! Shall I write to him?

CHICHIKOV: By all means!

PLYUSHKIN: And what a friend! We went to school together!

GOGOL: Suddenly a ray of warmth glided over those wooden features, an expression of—no, not emotion, but the reflection of emotion, like the face of a drowning man bobbing up unexpectedly in the water and whose emergence calls forth a joyous shout from those on the shore. But the rope is thrown in vain, the drowning man has come up for the last time. All is lost, and the still waters close again, even more fearful and desolate, over his body. So it was with Plyushkin's face.

PLYUSHKIN: (*Who has been rummaging.*) I had a clean sheet o'paper on this table; but my people are such a bunch of low-lifes. . . . Mavra, hey, Mavra!

(MAVRA *appears with a plate of cake covered in cobwebs, like Miss Havisham's.*)

PLYUSHKIN: Where did you hide that paper, you murderess?

MAVRA: Honest to God, master, I ain't laid eyes on that paper, 'cept a scrap you wipes your specs with.

PLYUSHKIN: I can tell by your face you sneaked off with it.

MAVRA: And what would I be wantin' paper fer? I cain't read nor write.

PLYUSHKIN: Liar! You took it to that sexton that's allus scribbling.

MAVRA: The sexton can get his own paper. He never laid eyes on your scraps.

PLYUSHKIN: Jest you wait till Doomsday, the devils'll make it hot for you with their pitchforks. Jest you wait and see!

MAVRA: Why should they make it hot for me, I never laid a finger on that paper!

PLYUSHKIN: Them devils'll say, "There, you sneak-thief," they'll say, "take that for cheatin' your master!" and they'll poke their red hot tools right into ya!

MAVRA: And I'll say, "You ain't got no call to do it! God is my judge, I din't take it." Why, there's yer old paper, right there on the table!

PLYUSHKIN: (*Gnawing his lips.*) Now, why fly off the handle, you touchy critter! Say one word to her and she comes back with ten. Now go get me somethin' to melt the sealin' wax. Hold on! Not a tallow candle; tallow'll be the ruin of me. You bring me a splinter of kindlin'. (MAVRA *exits.*)

(*Sits down, tears the paper into four pieces, and tries to write in as little space as possible.*)

GOGOL: Can a man sink to such insignificance, such pettiness? Is this at all likely? It is indeed. Any fiery youth in this assemblage would recoil in horror if he saw a portrait of himself in his old age. Take your humane impulses with you as you coarsen into manhood, or else the grave will be more merciful than your old age!

PLYUSHKIN: Do you have a friend, mebbe, who needs runaway souls?

CHICHIKOV: (*Quickly.*) You have runaways too?

PLYUSHKIN: Do I ever. 'Nigh onto seventy.

CHICHIKOV: No?

PLYUSHKIN: Gospel truth. Not a year goes by but some of 'em don't run off. My people are greedy pigs, stuffing their guts out o' idleness. So you tell your friend he can have 'em cheap.

CHICHIKOV: No, the legal fees are too expensive. But if you're so hard pressed, I'd be willing to give you, out of sympathy . . . oh, but it's such a trifle it's hardly worth talking about.

PLYUSHKIN: How much, how much? (*His hands start to quiver.*)

CHICHIKOV: Twenty kopeks per soul!

PLYUSHKIN: Spot cash?

CHICHIKOV: Spot cash.

PLYUSHKIN: Oh, kind sir, for the sake of my poverty, make it forty kopeks each.

CHICHIKOV: I can't! I might tack on another five kopeks. . . .

PLYUSHKIN: Tack 'em on, tack 'em on.

CHICHIKOV: Very well, how many runaways did you say? Seventy?

PLYUSHKIN: Eight and seventy.

CHICHIKOV: Eight and seventy at thirty kopeks apiece comes to . . . twenty-three rubles, forty kopeks.

GOGOL: He was strong in arithmetic.

(CHICHIKOV *pays the money into* PLYUSHKIN*'s trembling hands, which convey the cash to the bureau as if it were liquid brimming over.*)

PLYUSHKIN: (*As he escorts* CHICHIKOV *out*). Proshka! Take the Easter cake back to Mavra, we don't need it! Or better yet, I'll take it myself. Good-bye, dear sir! God bless you! (CHICHIKOV *gets in the carriage and drives off.*) What a man! I'll make him a present of my pocket-watch, it's a good watch, silver, out of order, true enough, but he can get it repaired. Or no, I'd better leave it to him in my will, to remember me by.

(*The carriage is riding along buoyantly,* CHICHIKOV *whistling merrily.*)

CHICHIKOV: A godsend, a gift! Over two hundred souls! And for a song! (*Whistles and imitates different instruments.*)

SELIFAN: (*Whipping up the horses.*) Eh, me hearties! Just you listen how the boss's singing! Oh, he's in a good mood today! He's on top o' the world!

[END OF PART ONE]

PART TWO

Episode 9

(CHICHIKOV *is snoring away in his bed in the inn.* GOGOL *is seated at his marble table at the Roman cafe.*)

GOGOL: (*Subdued.*) Happy the writer who can bypass characters that are tiresome, disgusting, and disturbing in their sad reality, and can snuggle up to characters that display human dignity. Happy the writer who can select the noble exceptions from the morass of everyday figures crowding in around him. He clouds men's eyes with incense and flatters their senses by concealing the seamy side of life and showing them Man as the Apex of All Creation. In return, men call him a poet for the ages, a sublime genius, unequalled in his power—he is God!

LUIGI: (*The waiter.*) Dante, Tasso, Homer, Virgil!

GOGOL: But that is not the lot of the writer who reveals what men are surrounded by at every moment and yet never see— that ghastly, slimy swamp of trivia that bogs down our life and lurks within the dreary swarms of humdrum characters. Such a writer will not win the plaudits of the crowd or even the hero-worship of a teen-aged girl. His style will be judged insignificant and his creations base. His course in life is austere, and bitterly he tastes his loneliness.

LUIGI: You 'ave 'nother grappa, Signor Gogol, make you feel better.

GOGOL: Yet I am fated by some wondrous power to proceed hand in hand with my strange heroes (*Rising from the table and moving to* CHICHIKOV.), to contemplate life in its entirety, amid the laughter that the world perceives but fails to appreciate, and the tears it does not perceive. Some day an awesome inspiration will thunder upon us, and mankind, abashed, will feel the majestic eloquence of . . .

(CHICHIKOV *snores especially loudly.*)

GOGOL: Well, let's get on with it! Away with melancholy! Let's plunge back into the folderol and jingle-jangle of life, and see what Chichikov is up to.

CHICHIKOV: (*Awakes, stretches.*) Petrushka!

PETRUSHKA: (*Enters, carrying his master's clothes.*) Here, master!

CHICHIKOV: Ugh, there's that smell again! Why don't you open the windows?

PETRUSHKA: (*Helping him into a dressing gown.*) I did open 'em.

CHICHIKOV: Liar. Never mind, I'm too happy to argue. Get my breakfast—something light, say a suckling pig.

(PETRUSHKA *exits.*)

CHICHIKOV: (*His face lights up.*) I own four hundred souls! (*Snaps his fingers.*) How about that! (*Looks in the mirror and feels his chin.*) Look at that, what a chin, it's perfectly round! (*Leaps around the room, slapping his buttocks with his heels.*) Time to get down to business. (*Sits at the table and pulls papers out of his little casket.* PETRUSHKA *enters with tea and crullers.*) Here's Korobochka's list. Why, she's given each peasant a nickname. And here's Plyushkin's. He doesn't waste words—or anything else: They're all abbreviated. And Sobakevich's—lots of information here. "A good carpenter." "Knows his work and doesn't touch alcohol." Good grief, what a horde of you are crowded in here! What did you do in your lifetime? "Pyotr Never-Minds-the-Pig-Sty!" What a long fellow you are, sprawled over a whole line! What carried you off? Were you run over by a cart as you slept off a drunk in the middle of the road? (*The light changes, folk music is faintly heard, and as* CHICHIKOV *speculates*

EPISODE 9

the various peasants appear in idealized form and act out what he describes.)

CHICHIKOV: Corky Stepan—Carpenter: of exemplary sobriety. Oh, yes, the very tall fellow! Strode through the land with his axe stuck in his belt and his boots slung over his shoulder, I'll bet. How did you die? Did you clamber up a scaffold to plant a cross on the church-tower, slip on a plank, and smash against the ground, with only Uncle Mikhey to stand by and say:

UNCLE MIKHEY: (*Scratching his neck.*) You had to go and do it, din't ya?

CHICHIKOV: Maiksm Telyatnikov, shoemaker. Drunk as a cobbler too, I'll be bound! You stocked rotten leather and all the boots you made split and cracked, so your little shop was abandoned by customers and you started taking a nip now and again and traipsing round the streets, saying:

MAKSIM TELYATNIKOV: Oh, it's a bad world! You can't make a living if you're a Russian. Them damn furriners won't let you!

CHICHIKOV: Grigory Try-and-get-there-but-you-won't! What sort were you? Did your friends bump you off, quarreling over some apple-cheeked soldier's wife? Or did some tramp lurking in the forest do you in for your warm mittens? Or did you get to thinking and thinking and finally dive right through a hole in the ice? Ah, Russians! They don't like dying a natural death. What the hell's this? Elizabethus Sparrow! That goddamn Sobakevich! He slipped in a wench by giving her name a masculine ending! (*And, sure enough, one of the peasants removes his beard to reveal himself a woman.*) Cross her off, cross her off. Oh, and Plyushkin's runaways, who might just as well be dead. Are you roaming and robbing or wasting away in jail? Popov, a domestic . . . probably could read and write. Wouldn't take a knife to anybody but would steal in a nice genteel way. Probably nabbed by a Rural Police Captain by now for not having what he'd call a "pashport."

POLICE CAPTAIN: (*With each question manhandles* POPOV *a different way.*) Who do you belong to?

POPOV: Ivan Ivanovich Ivanov! Oryol province!

POLICE CAPTAIN: What are you doing here then?

POPOV: He's give me a leave of absence.

POLICE CAPTAIN: Where's your pashport?

POPOV: With the master that hired me, Pimenov.

POLICE CAPTAIN: He says no. Why are you lying?

POPOV: That's right. I didn't give it to him, 'cause I got home late, so I gave it for safe-keeping to Antip Prokhorov the bell-ringer.

POLICE CAPTAIN: Lying again! Where is your pashport?

POPOV: I did have it, but I must have dropped it on the road somewheres.

POLICE CAPTAIN: And what about that soldier's overcoat you swiped? And the poorbox from the church?

POPOV: I don't know. I never stole nothing. Somebody must have planted that stuff on me.

POLICE CAPTAIN: You filthy swine! Clap him in leg-irons and put him behind bars!

POPOV: I'll go with pleasure! (*Looking round.*) Hmph! I been in cleaner prisons than this, and roomier. No place for sports here.

CHICHIKOV: Avvakum Fyrov! And are you living free and easy, as a barge-hauler along the Volga? Making merry with ribbons in your hat, dancing in a ring and singing songs, before you have to toil and sweat, hauling the tow-rope to the strain of a song endless in all Russia! (*The strains of "Ay ukhnyem!" (The Volga Boat Song) are interrupted by a clock striking. All the peasants vanish.*) Twelve o'clock! What a fool I am! It's about time I did something useful!

Episode 10

(CHICHIKOV, *aided by* PETRUSHKA, *dresses and starts out with his documents. As he does so,* GOGOL *explains:*)

EPISODE 10   65

GOGOL: Chichikov was hurrying not because he was afraid of being late. Rather, he hoped to wind up the matter as quickly as he could, for despite it all, he entertained the feeling that his souls were not quite the genuine article, and, in such cases, it is best to get things over with as soon as possible.

MANILOV: (*In a cap with earlaps, and kid gloves.*) Pavel Ivanovich! (CHICHIKOV *and* MANILOV *embrace tightly and exchange kisses. Clinging to* CHICHIKOV's *hand:*) I flew to town on the wings of friendship to clasp you to my bosom.

GOGOL: His speech concluded with a compliment appropriate only to some dainty damsel one is about to lead in a dance.

CHICHIKOV: I hardly know how to thank . . .

MANILOV: (*Producing a scroll tied with a pink ribbon.*) Voilà!

CHICHIKOV: What's this?

MANILOV: Those dear little peasants.

CHICHIKOV: Aha! (*Unrolls it and admires.*) Exquisite. Why, there's even a border around it! Whoever made such a cunning border?

MANILOV: (*Blushing.*) You mustn't ask.

CHICHIKOV: Was it you?

MANILOV: My wife.

CHICHIKOV: Dear me, I really feel guilty for causing you so much trouble.

MANILOV: No trouble at all, where Pavel Ivanovich is concerned. (CHICHIKOV *bows.*) Now I know you're off to the Town Hall to see the title-deeds executed. I insist on accompanying you. (*They link arms and start off,* MANILOV *murmuring endearments and helping* CHICHIKOV *over every little bump: "You mustn't stub your dear toes," etc.*)

GOGOL: At the Town Hall, our heroes beheld a vast amount of frock coats and tailcoats and one light gray jacket which, with its head twisted to one side and all but resting on the paper, was deftly copying out the inventory of an estate appropriated from some placid landowner who had lived long enough to beget both children and grandchildren during the time the benign lawsuit had dragged on.

FIRST CLERK: (*In a whisky tenor.*) Feodosey Feodosyev, bring me file 368!

SECOND CLERK: Where do you always hide the top to the ink-bottle?

OFFICIAL: (*Majestically.*) Copy that out! If it's not done in time, I'll confiscate your boots and keep you here for a week without food.

(*Noise of scratching of quills, making the sound of heavy-laden carts driving through dry leaves.*)

CHICHIKOV: (*To* FIRST CLERK.) Excuse me, where are peasant matters dealt with?

CLERKS: (*In unison.*) Just what's your business?

CHICHIKOV: Why, I have to formalize a sale.

CLERKS: Just what have you bought?

CHICHIKOV: First I want to know which desk handles peasants: is it here or somewhere else?

CLERKS: Yes, but first, tell us what you bought and what you paid, and then we'll tell you where to go.

CHICHIKOV: Look, if you know the proper desk, tell me. Otherwise, I'll tell *you* where to go.

(FIRST CLERK *jabs a finger toward an old codger shuffling papers in a corner.*)

CHICHIKOV: (*Bowing to* CODGER.) May I ask if this is the desk for peasant matters?

CODGER: (*Very slowly.*) Peasants are handled elsewhere.

CHICHIKOV: Where then?

CODGER: You want the Department of Peasants.

EPISODE 10   67

CHICHIKOV: And which is the Department of Peasants?

CODGER: That's run by Ivan Antonovich.

CHICHIKOV: And where is Ivan Antonovich?

(CODGER *jabs a finger in another direction.* IVAN ANTONOVICH, *a man whose face is mostly nose, sees them coming out of the corner of his eye and plunges deep into writing.*)

CHICHIKOV: Excuse me, is this the Department of Peasants? (IVAN ANTONOVICH *burrows deeper into papers.*) I said, is this the Department of Peasants?

IVAN ANTONOVICH: (*Without ceasing.*) Yes.

CHICHIKOV: Well, here's my business: I have bought from various local landowners some serfs I wish to resettle elsewhere. The deeds of sale are made out—they just have to be certified.

IVAN ANTONOVICH: Are the sellers here in person?

CHICHIKOV: Some are, and I have proxy letters from the others.

IVAN ANTONOVICH: And you've brought the application with you?

CHICHIKOV: Of course. I would like . . . I'm in rather a hurry . . . so could the business be settled today?

IVAN ANTONOVICH: What! Today? . . . Out of the question . . . Title-searches have to be made, and so on.

CHICHIKOV: Well, if it comes to that, your Bureau Chief is a good friend of mine. . . .

IVAN ANTONOVICH: (*Sternly.*) He's not the only one around here.

CHICHIKOV: The others won't be left out. I was a public servant myself. I know how things are done. (CHICHIKOV *takes out a bank note and puts it on the desk.* IVAN ANTONOVICH *absently covers it with a ledger and nods.*)

IVAN ANTONOVICH: (*Thawing.*) Then have the Bureau Chief issue the order through the proper channels and we'll see it's taken care of. I'll escort you to the Bureau Chief's office. (IVAN ANTONOVICH *escorts* CHICHIKOV *and* MANILOV *to the office, where* BUREAU CHIEF *and* SOBAKEVICH *are waiting. Embraces, kisses, and salutations among all except* SOBAKEVICH, *whose presence slightly disconcerts* CHICHIKOV.)

CHICHIKOV: (*Somewhat sheepishly to* SOBAKEVICH.) And how's your health?

SOBAKEVICH: Nothing to complain about, thank God. (*Sighing.*) Imagine, I'm getting on in years and I haven't been sick a day in my life—not so much as a sore throat or a boil on my bottom. . . . That's a bad sign! I'll pay for it sooner or later.

CHICHIKOV: (*To* BUREAU CHIEF.) What a man! Look what he decides to complain about. Oh, by the way, I have a note for you.

BUREAU CHIEF: Who from? (*Reading it.*) Ah, Plyushkin! So he's still vegetating. . . . What a fate! Once he was such an intelligent, prosperous man . . . and now!

SOBAKEVICH: A dirty dog. A crook. He starves all his serfs to death.

BUREAU CHIEF: (*Having read the note.*) By all means. I'll be glad to act as his proxy. Do you want to execute the deed of sale now or later?

CHICHIKOV: Now. Today, if it's at all possible, because I'd like to leave town tomorrow.

BUREAU CHIEF: Well, you can conclude your business today, but you'll still have to tarry with us a while. Here, Ivan Antonovich, take all these deeds of sale for this gentleman.

SOBAKEVICH: Don't forget, you'll need witnesses for each party. Send for the Public Prosecutor; he's probably lounging at home right now. And the Postmaster's a loafer too, you'll find him at home if he hasn't traipsed off to play cards. And there's lots of others, Dandruffsky, Putrefactov, they just clutter up the earth.

BUREAU CHIEF: Quite so, quite so! Ivan Antonovich, will you please round up some witnesses! (IVAN ANTONOVICH *starts off.*) We'll attend to everything. And as for clerks, don't give them a thing, please! Friends of mine don't pay! (IVAN ANTONOVICH *turns around with a baleful look.* CHICHIKOV *shakes his head with a smile and* IVAN ANTONOVICH *leaves sullenly.*) So you've made some acquisitions, Pavel Ivanovich!

CHICHIKOV: I have indeed.

BUREAU CHIEF: Good for you!

CHICHIKOV: Best thing I could have done. After all, a man's goal in life is vague until he's got a firm footing and given up the free-thinking fantasies of youth. The young are too liberal-minded, too. . . . (*Catches* SOBAKEVICH*'s eye and coughs in embarrassment.*)

SOBAKEVICH: Why don't you tell Ivan Grigorievich just what you've acquired? The serfs he bought! Solid gold! Why, I even sold him Mikheyev the coachmaker.

BUREAU CHIEF: No! Really? You sold him Mikheyev? Why, he's a master craftsman, fixed my carriage for me. But wait . . . didn't you tell me he died?

SOBAKEVICH: Mikheyev dead? Bosh! His brother it was that died. Mikheyev's in the pink. A few days ago he built a coach that couldn't be bettered in Moscow. Work fit for the Tsar.

BUREAU CHIEF: Yes, a master craftsman. I wonder you were willing to part with him.

SOBAKEVICH: And not just Mikheyev! Corky Stepan, my carpenter, and Milushkin, my brick-layer, and Telyatnikov my shoemaker! I sold every last one of them!

BUREAU CHIEF: But why?

SOBAKEVICH: (*With a wave of the hand.*) Came down with a dumbness attack. Sell 'em, I said, and sell 'em I did, fool that I am! (*Hanging his head repentantly.*) Gray hair on top, no wits inside.

BUREAU CHIEF: (*To* CHICHIKOV.) But, Pavel Ivanovich, how come you're buying serfs without land?

CHICHIKOV: For resettlement.

BUREAU CHIEF: I see . . . and whereabouts will you resettle them?

CHICHIKOV: Whereabouts? . . . Kherson province.

BUREAU CHIEF: Oh, that's fine land. Have you enough?

CHICHIKOV: Enough for the number of peasants I've bought.

BUREAU CHIEF: With a river or a pond?

CHICHIKOV: A river. But there's a pond too. (*Catches* SOBAKEVICH's *eye and coughs again.*)

(IVAN ANTONOVICH *ushers in the witnesses: the* PUBLIC PROSECUTOR, *the* POSTMASTER, *the* CHIEF OF POLICE, *the* SANITATION INSPECTOR, *etc.*)

BUREAU CHIEF: Gentlemen! I've asked you here to witness the transaction of some deeds of sale. Our friend Pavel Ivanovich has made some remarkable acquisitions!

(*Embraces, salutations, congratulations. The witnesses huddle to sign papers* IVAN ANTONOVICH *passes around.*)

SOBAKEVICH: (*Whispering to* CHICHIKOV.) And why did you buy souls from Plyushkin?

CHICHIKOV: And why did you tack Sparrow on your list?

SOBAKEVICH: What Sparrow?

CHICHIKOV: The peasant woman Elizabeth Sparrow—you wrote her name Elizabethus.

SOBAKEVICH: I never tacked on no sparrow. (*He walks away to sign.*)

IVAN ANTONOVICH: (*Passing* CHICHIKOV *with the signed papers.*) You bought a hundred thousand worth of serfs, and all you've given me for my work is a measly twenty-five rubles.

CHICHIKOV: If you knew the kind of serfs they were! (IVAN ANTONOVICH *exits, disgruntled.*)

BUREAU CHIEF: And now, gentlemen, all that's left is to baptize the bargain.

CHICHIKOV: I'm agreeable. I'll be happy to stand to a bottle or two of bubbly.

BUREAU CHIEF: Oh no, it's up to us to treat you to bubbly!

CHIEF OF POLICE: You're our guest. Leave it to me!

POSTMASTER: Our Chief of Police is a miracle-worker.

SANITATION INSPECTOR: Treats the grocers' shops like his own pantry.

(CHIEF OF POLICE *claps his hands and* CLERKS *bring in food and drink.*)

GOGOL: Lo and behold! the table was laden with salted sturgeon (the white kind), salted sturgeon (the ordinary kind), smoked and pickled salmon, caviar both pressed and freshly salted, herrings, a third kind of sturgeon (stellated), cheese, smoked tongue, and dried sturgeon fillets; a fish-head pie, a pepper-mushroom pie, fritters, dumplings fried in butter, and dumplings boiled.

(*The witnesses begin to eat and drink spiritedly;* SOBAKEVICH *makes off with a whole sturgeon and sits to one side, devouring it.*)

POSTMASTER: (*Raising a glass.*) To the health of our new Kherson landowner!

CHIEF OF POLICE: (*Ditto.*) To the successful resettlement of his peasants!

BUREAU CHIEF: (*Ditto*). To the health of his lovely bride-to-be!

CHICHIKOV: How's that?

BUREAU CHIEF: No, Pavel Ivanovich! Say what you like, but we'll marry you off!

SANITATION INSPECTOR: We'll find you a beautiful, well-endowed bride! Won't we, gentlemen?

CHIEF OF POLICE: You can fight hand and foot, but it won't do you any good! We'll marry you off just the same!

CHICHIKOV: Why should I resist hand and foot? But after all, marriage isn't just one of those things. . . . You've got to come up with a bride first!

BUREAU CHIEF: Don't you worry about that! We'll find one!

CHIEF OF POLICE: We'll find you whatever you like!

CHICHIKOV: Well, in that case—

(*Laughter, clinking of glasses. They press in around* CHICHIKOV, *congratulating and embracing. The noise increases, they start to do folk dances around him.* CHICHIKOV, *tipsy, gets up on a chair.*)

CHICHIKOV: (*Over the racket.*) I've got every intention of introducing improvements on my land, scientific rotation of crops and so on, to make the place fit for my bride, for, after all, what can be more blissful than the happiness of two souls who share an affinity, right Anton Antonovich? (MANILOV *smiles wanly.*)—remember young Werther's epistle to Charlotte, how does it go?

SANITATION OFFICIAL: Dear Charlotte . . .

CHICHIKOV: (*To* SOBAKEVICH.) Surely you remember your Goethe, Mikhail Semyonovich . . . (*He steps off the chair as if to go to* SOBAKEVICH *but is caught in midflight by the others. They carry him over to* SELIFAN, *who collects him and drives him to the inn, holding the reins in one hand and supporting his master with the other.* PETRUSHKA *puts him to bed. During this commotion,* MANILOV *and* SOBAKEVICH *make off, leaving only the* OFFICIALS, *who get progressively drunker during the next scene. They sing and hum the folk song* "Slender Mountain Ash" (*"Tonkaya ryabina."*).)

SANITATION INSPECTOR: I repeat, lands in our southern provinces may be rich and fertile, but there are no rivers or ponds. And peasants without water . . .

CHIEF OF POLICE: (*Laughing.*) Are like fish out of water!

BUREAU CHIEF: Water shortage doesn't mean a thing, not a

EPISODE 10

thing. It's resettlement itself that's the problem. You know what peasants are like: they'll run off as sure as two and two make . . . four.

CHIEF OF POLICE: (*Waltzing.*) Don't blame me, gentlemen. I offered Chichikov a millinery escort, you were all nitwesses, gentlemen, but he turned me down flat!

POSTMASTER: No, hold on, hold on, Chichikov's peasants won't run off. A Russian can adapt to anything, no matter the climate. You can even send him to Siberia and if you give him warm mittens, he'll take an axe and start building a new cabin.

PUBLIC PROSECUTOR: But you've left out one important factor: what kind of peasants has he bought? No landowner will sell a good serf.

CHIEF OF POLICE: Right!

PUBLIC PROSECUTOR: I'll stake my head that the serfs Chichikov has bought are thieves and vagabonds, drunkards and roughnecks.

SANITATION INSPECTOR: Quite so, quite so; but the moral to that is: Once these good-for-nothings are settled in a new land, they may become decent people in no time at all.

PUBLIC PROSECUTOR: Never, never! Chichikov's peasants have two powerful enemies to contend with. First, the province is licensed to sell liquor and in two weeks they'll drink themselves blind.

POSTMASTER: (*Slipping on to the floor.*) Dreadful, dreadful!

PUBLIC PROSECUTOR: The second enemy is Wanderlust.

CHIEF OF POLICE: Wanda who?

BUREAU CHIEF: Lust!

PUBLIC PROSECUTOR: Chichikov had better treat them with an iron fist . . .

CHIEF OF POLICE: With his own two fists. The old one-two—knock a peasant's teeth out or plant a good solid clout on his neck.

POSTMASTER: A sacred obligation lies ahead of Chichikov. He should become a, so to speak, father to his peasants.

CHIEF OF POLICE: That's enough of that, Ivan Andreich-Sprechen-Sie-Deutsch!

POSTMASTER: History is full of examples!

CHIEF OF POLICE: History is full of . . .

BUREAU CHIEF: Gentlemen, let us abandon these idle speculations and . . . and . . . with another little glass of vodka toast the health . . .

SANITATION INSPECTOR: Of Chichikov's industrious peasants! Hear, hear!

(*They raise their glasses. The lights dim. The toasting turns into a cacophonous babble of talk.*)

Episode 11

(*The babble of voices becomes exclusively feminine, and* ANNA GRIGORIEVNA *and* SOFIYA IVANOVNA *emerge.*)

ANNA GRIGORIEVNA: My dear, the fact is, he's a millionaire!

SOFIYA IVANOVNA: A millionaire, at the very least!

GOVERNOR'S WIFE: (*Putting in an appearance.*) We must throw a ball in his honor! (*Various other ladies appear, chattering excitedly.*)

GOGOL: The ladies of this town were . . . no, I'm just not up to it, I don't dare. The most remarkable thing about the ladies of the town was . . . it's very odd, my tongue refuses to move. I'll keep it to a few words. The ladies of the town were what is called—presentable. They were distinguished by an exceptional regard for decorum. Never would you hear them say:

SERF WENCH: I gotta blow my nose.

Episode 11

GOGOL: Or . . .

SERF WENCH: I gotta spit.

GOGOL: Instead they would say:

ANNA GRIGORIEVNA: I must relieve my nostrils.

SOFIYA IVANOVNA: I am constrained to deploy my handkerchief.

GOGOL: Under no circumstances would they say:

SERF WENCH: This glass stinks.

GOGOL: Instead, they would say something like:

GOVERNOR'S WIFE: This glass is being very, very naughty.

GOGOL: And further to aggrandize the Russian language, they had frequent recourse to a French vocabulary.

ANNA GRIGORIEVNA: *Precisément! Ce qu'on appèle un MILLIONAIRE!*

SOFIYA IVANOVNA: *Vraiment, ma chère,* this Chichikov is not *l'homme le plus beau au monde!*

ANNA GRIGORIEVNA: Perhaps not, but he's all that a man should be!

SOFIYA IVANOVNA: Don't you find him just the teensiest bit inclined to *embonpoint.*

ANNA GRIGORIEVNA: Thin men, my dear, more closely resemble toothpicks than human beings.

GOGOL: Chichikov could not help but notice the feminine interest in his appearance. As a result, his looks became even more amiable, his collars snowier, and he sported a new watch-chain. He became seductive. (*As the* INN SERVANT.) Two letters for you, sir!

CHICHIKOV: (*Opening one.*) Ah, an invitation to a ball at the Governor's! (*Opening the other.*) And what's this? "No, I positively must write to you! There is a mysterious affinity of souls . . ." (*To* INN SERVANT.) Who brought this?

GOGOL/INN SERVANT: A servant brought it, said the party wanted to remain unknownymous.

CHICHIKOV: "Affinity of souls dot dot dot."

FEMALE VOICE-OVER: What is our life? A vale of sorrows! What is the world? A senseless herd of creatures. I am bedewing with tears the following lines written by my sainted mother—who passed away twenty-five years ago. Oh, dear Pavel Ivanovich, visit me in my wilderness, abandon the stifling cities where one cannot breathe fresh air.
Two mourning doves are here to show
The place where lie my bones;
Their lovesick cooing lets you know
I did expire with tears and groans.

CHICHIKOV: Funny meter, that. No matter. No signature either. Hm, a P.S.

FEMALE VOICE-OVER: Your heart should divine the writer of these lines, who will be present on the morrow at the Governor's ball.

CHICHIKOV: Well, well, well! Petrushka! Lay out my best clothes! (*On one side of the stage,* CHICHIKOV *shaves, contemplates his face in the mirror, smiles and bows, winks and clacks his tongue, as he dresses and finally cuts a caper. Meanwhile on the other side of the stage,* KOROBOCHKA*'s carriage enters.*)

GOGOL: While Chichikov was bedizening himself for the ball and night was peeping into windows, in another part of town our hero's fate was about to be severely altered.

CHICHIKOV: (*In the mirror.*) You heartbreaker, you!

GOGOL: Through the remote bypaths of the town an odd vehicle lumbered joltingly along: It resembled nothing so much as a bulging watermelon on wheels, and was filled to the bursting with calico pillows, loaves of bread, biscuits, and two pies, one chicken and one corned beef.

CHICHIKOV: Wonder what the Governor's chef will give us for supper? A hazel-grouse with mayonnaise or a cold sturgeon with truffles and capers!

EPISODE 11   77

GOGOL: The horses kept stumbling, owing to their unfamiliarity with the roads and the fact that they had no shoes. This antediluvian rattletrap finally turned into a sidestreet by the church of St. Nicholas-in-the-Sticks, and stopped before the house of the priest.

CHICHIKOV: Balls are wonderful things! The crops may have failed, or the weather's freezing, but when people gather for a party they forget their troubles. Something for everyone: dancing for the young folks, cards for those who've reached the age of discretion. Everything's merry and bright!

GOGOL: A wench in a kerchief crawled out and began pounding on the gate as hard as any *man* could. Dogs barked and at last the gaping gates swallowed up the cumbersome conveyance.

CHICHIKOV: Oh, the world's a marvelous place, damn it all! I love everybody!

KOROBOCHKA: (*Emerging from the carriage.*) How much are dead souls going for!?

(*Rapid blackout on both* CHICHIKOV *and* KOROBOCHKA. *Sudden blaze of lights. A galopade is going full blast at the ball, featuring* SOFIYA IVANOVNA, *the* RURAL POLICE CAPTAIN, *a lady with a blue plume, a lady with a white plume, a Frenchman named Coucou (played by* GOGOL), *the Georgian Prince Chipkhaikhilidzay. Dandruffsky, etc., all whirling around.*)

CHICHIKOV: (*Entering.*) Here we go! The whole province is on the move.

(*Spotting* CHICHIKOV, *the guests, including all the* OFFICIALS, *cluster around him.*)

GOVERNOR: (*Dropping a poodle he had been holding.*) Pavel Ivanovich!

(*Ad libbing:* "Ah, dear me, it's Pavel Ivanovich!" "Dear Pavel Ivanovich!" "Darling Pavel Ivanovich!" "Most esteemed Pavel Ivanovich!" "Here you are at last, Pavel Ivanovich!" "Let me embrace you, Pavel Ivanovich!" "Send him over here: I want to give Pavel Ivanovich a nice big kiss!")

CHICHIKOV: (*Bowing to all and sundry.*) Most charmed, delighted! Good evening! (*To the ladies.*) How lovely! What perfumes! This is no province, this is the metropolis! Paris itself! (*Chorus of charmed approval.*) (*Extricating himself; aside.*) I wonder which one of them wrote the letter?

ANNA GRIGORIEVNA: Then you approve of our ladies, Pavel Ivanovich?

CHICHIKOV: How can I help it?

SOFIYA IVANOVNA: And how would you describe them, Pavel Ivanovich?

CHICHIKOV: How can you convey all those subtle nuances that flit over a woman's face, the light in her eyes, melting, velvety, languishing, voluptuous . . .

LADIES: (*Teased and tickled.*) Ooooh!

CHICHIKOV: That light will snatch at your heart and strum on it like a fiddle bow, plucking at every chord of your soul.

LADIES: (*In ecstasy.*) Ooh!

CHICHIKOV: No, there's no way to describe it! Women are . . . women are . . . the fancy-pants half of humanity!

LADIES: (*Shocked.*) Oh! (*They withdraw a bit.*)

GOVERNOR'S WIFE: (*Coming up.*) Ah, Pavel Ivanovich, can it be that others have so taken possession of your heart, that there is not the tiniest nook for those you have so ruthlessly neglected?

CHICHIKOV: (*Mincing.*) Dear lady, I . . . (*Stops in amazement as he sees the* GOVERNOR'S DAUGHTER. *A clap of thundeer freezes him in place.*)

GOVERNOR'S WIFE: You haven't been introduced to my daughter yet, have you? She's just finished finishing school.

CHICHIKOV: I . . . I have had the good fortune to encounter her on the road . . . our carriages collid . . . some peasants . . .

EPISODE 11   79

GOVERNOR DAUGHTER: (*With a casual curtsy.*) How do? (*The* GOVERNOR'S WIFE *and* DAUGHTER *move off into the crowd.*)

CHICHIKOV: I'm so . . . (*Trails off, frozen in place, following them with his eyes.*)

ANNA GRIGORIEVNA: May we poor mortals make so bold as to inquire whither your reveries tend?

SOFIYA IVANOVNA: What is the location of those happy regions where your thoughts take wing?

LADY IN WHITE PLUME: May one know the name of the fair one who has plunged you into this dulcet vale of pensiveness?

(CHICHIKOV, *like an automaton, walks straight across the room to the* GOVERNOR'S DAUGHTER.)

LADIES: Well, I never! Can you imagine! Of all the nerve!

(*A mazurka has started up. In following the* GOVERNOR'S DAUGHTER *through the mazes of the dance,* CHICHIKOV *keeps bumping into dancers and getting in the way. Some of the lady dancers throw him killing glances as he passes, but when he ignores them they get huffy. Finally the* GOVERNOR'S DAUGHTER *sits on a divan, and* CHICHIKOV *haltingly sits beside her.*)

GOGOL: (*As he dances during the mazurka.*) It's hard to say whether the emotion of love had truly arisen in our hero's breast. Can such run-of-the-mill gentlemen fall in love? And yet, something strange and inexplicable deafened him to the caterwauling of the music and the chatter of the guests, and blinded him to all except the ivory-colored, translucent, radiant simplicity of the Governor's daughter.

CHICHIKOV: My dear young lady, I really must compliment you on the egg-like purity of your toilette.

GOVERNOR'S DAUGHTER: (*Giggles.*)

CHICHIKOV: (*Disconcerted*) Vast as is this realm of ours, this Russia, yet that we, by sheer coincidence, should meet in so inadvertant a way . . . Why, I was just saying, the last time I was in Simbirsk at the home of Sofron Ivanovich Bezpechny, to his daughter Adelaida and his three sisters-in-law Mariya Gavrilovna, Aleksandra Gavrilovna and Adelheida Gavrilovna . . .

(ANNA IVANOVNA *purposely brushes against them to flutter her scarf in the* GOVERNOR'S DAUGHTER*'s face.*)

CHICHIKOV: (*Progressively more distraught.*) I am sorry, I mean the house of Fyodor Fyodorovich Perekroev in Ryazan province, when I said to his sister-in-law Katerina Mikhailovna and her second cousins Rosa Fyodorovna and Emilia Fyodorovna . . .

GOVERNOR'S DAUGHTER: (*Yawns.*)

SOFIYA IVANOVNA: (*Cattily, in passing.*) What a brilliant conversationalist!

CHICHIKOV: (*Rambling on despite himself.*) Frol Vasilievich Pobedonosov, his brother Pyotr Vasilievich, Pyotr Varsonofoevich, his daughter-in-law's sister Pelageya Egorovna, Sofiya Rostislavna and her two stepsisters . . .

GOVERNOR'S DAUGHTER: (*Yawns continuously during this.*)

LADY IN WHITE PLUME: (*Over* CHICHIKOV'S *rambling.*) Millionaire he may be, but he certainly wants manners!

SOFIYA IVANOVNA: I don't see why you think he's got a military bearing!

CHICHIKOV: Sofiya Aleksandrovna and Confetti Aleksandrovna . . .

ANNA GRIGORIEVNA: You were the one who called him Marslike!

SOFIYA IVANOVNA: I did not! I said he looked like a Martian!

CHICHIKOV: Anyway, as the Greek philosopher Diogenes used to say . . .

NOZDRYOV: (*Bursting in, laughing.*) Ah, the Kherson landowner! The Kherson landowner!

CHICHIKOV: (*Rising abruptly.*) Oh, my God! (*He tries to escape in the opposite direction and bumps into the* GOVERNOR.)

EPISODE 11   81

GOVERNOR: Ah, I've found you again! Delighted! You must come and settle a dispute between these ladies!

LADY IN WHITE PLUME: Do tell us, Pavel Ivanovich, is a man's love lasting or not?

ANNA GRIGORIEVNA: *(Caustically.)* Hah!

NOZDRYOV: *(Shoving his way through to* CHICHIKOV.*)* Hey, how's the dead souls business going? Hey, Governor, you hear about that? This fellow deals in dead souls!

ALL: *(In a whisper.)* Dead souls!

NOZDRYOV: Swear to God, he does! Say, Chichikov—let me say in true friendship, for we're all your friends here—the Governor is too—why, I'd string you up to the first tree that came along, swear to God, I would!

(The music has stopped. A hush has fallen on the assemblage. Everyone is astonished; CHICHIKOV *is dazed. Each time* NOZDRYOV *says "Dead souls," the assemblage repeats it somewhat more loudly.)*

NOZDRYOV: Would you believe it Governor, when he said to me, "Sell me some dead souls," I almost croaked laughing. Mizhuev—you know my brother-in-law Mizhuev?—tells me Chichikov bought three millions' worth of serfs to resettle. What serfs? What resettlement! They're all dead souls! Oh, Chichikov, you're a bastard, honest to God! Am I right, Prosecutor?

*(*PUBLIC PROSECUTOR *tries to say something, but* NOZDRYOV *forges ahead.)*

NOZDRYOV: No, no, no, brother . . . I won't go till you tell me why you were buying dead souls! You ought to be ashamed of yourself, I'm the best friend you've got . . . me and the Governor here. Right, Prosecutor? You can't believe how attached we are to each other. If you asked me which I loved better: My father or Chichikov? I'd say Chichikov! Lemme give you a kiss. Don't resist, Chichikov, let me plant one juicy little *baiser* on your snow-white cheek!

(CHICHIKOV *pushes him so hard* NOZDRYOV *falls back on to the assembled guests, who had been creeping up in a tight knot. They all fall to the floor, like dominos.*)

NOZDRYOV: Dead souls! He was buying dead souls!

CHIEF OF POLICE: Bah! Everyone knows Nozdryov's a chronic liar!

GOVERNOR: Of course, he's always talking nonsense.

ANNA GRIGORIEVNA: (*With a malicious smile.*) It's just a vulgar lie.

SOFIYA IVANOVNA: Underserving of any attention whatsoever. (*Smirks.*)

(*Murmuring "Lies! Dead souls!" the guests rise and swirl offstage.*)

CHICHIKOV: May the Devil take the man who invented balls!

[BLACKOUT]

Episode 12

GOGOL: As ill luck would have it, the next day our hero took to his bed with a sore throat and a gumboil, and decided to keep to his room lest, God forbid, he should somehow be terminated without leaving any offspring. (*He remains on stage throughout the next episodes.*) But that very morning a lady paid a call to another lady in the town. They shall remain nameless, because whatever name you come up with, somebody here is bound to protest I'm picking on her personally. Therefore, to avoid such an annoyance, let us call the lady on whom the visit was paid (ANNA GRIGORIEVNA *appears.*) "a lady agreeable in every respect," and her visitor (SOFIYA IVANOVNA *appears*), whose personality did not have so many facets, "a simply agreeable lady."

(ANNA GRIGORIEVNA *and* SOFIYA IVANOVNA *run at each other, scream, grab each other's hands, kiss, scream again, kiss loudly again.*)

Episode 12

ANNA GRIGORIEVNA: Come over here, in this little nook. Here's a cushion. Oh, I'm so glad it's you . . . I heard somebody drive up and I thought, who could it be so early? Not that cow the Governor's wife! and I was going to say—Oh, what a cheerful little print!

SOFIYA IVANOVNA: Yes, it is awfully cheerful, though Praskoviya Fyodorovna thinks it'd be better if the checks were a trifle smaller and the polka dots were blue. I just sent my sisters some bewitching material: itsy-bitsy little stripes, with a pattern of peepers and paws, peepers and paws, peepers and paws all over it. One of a kind!

ANNA GRIGORIEVNA: But, my dear, that's so loud!

SOFIYA IVANOVNA: No it's not!

ANNA GRIGORIEVNA: But it is!

SOFIYA IVANOVNA: Incidentally, flounces are out. (ANNA GRIGORIEVNA *is covered in flounces.*)

ANNA GRIGORIEVNA: Are they?

SOFIYA IVANOVNA: Little scallops are in—on sleeves, shoulders, skirts, scallops galore! It's darling!

ANNA GRIGORIEVNA: You may do what you choose, but I have no intention of following that fashion.

SOFIYA IVANOVNA: Neither do I . . . fashions get so extreme these days . . . Oh my God! I completely forgot. Do you know why I came here?

ANNA GRIGORIEVNA: About that Prince Charming of yours? Sing his praises to your heart's content, but I'll tell him to his face he's tacky, tacky, tacky!

SOFIYA IVANOVNA: But do listen to what I've got to say—

ANNA GRIGORIEVNA: Rumors to the contrary, he is not a human being, not a bit of it; and as for his nose . . . it's hateful.

SOFIYA IVANOVNA: (*Desperately imploring.*) Please, please, dearest darling, just let me tell you. Why, this is a regular affair! *Ce qu'on appelle affaire!*

ANNA GRIGORIEVNA: What affair?

SOFIYA IVANOVNA: Why, my treasure, just imagine: The Priest's wife came to me this morning and what do you think? Our fine visitor with his butter-wouldn't-melt-in-his-mouth ways, what sort of a fellow do you think he is?

ANNA GRIGORIEVNA: Don't tell me he's been trying to seduce the Priest's wife too?

SOFIYA IVANOVNA: Oh, if that were all. . . . The Priest's wife told me that a certain landowner, she says, a Mrs Korobochka, arrived scared out of her wits, with a story to tell. At the dead of night, she says, there's a terrific banging on her gates and a shout of: "Open up, open up, or I'll blow your gates down!" What sort of Prince Charming do you call that?

ANNA GRIGORIEVNA: Who's this Korobochka? Young, good-looking?

SOFIYA IVANOVNA: Hardly. An old crone.

ANNA GRIGORIEVNA: Oh charming! Now he's into raping old women!

SOFIYA IVANOVNA: You're way off the mark, Anna Grigorievna. Listen! Chichikov stands there armed to the teeth shouting, "Sell me all your dead souls."

ANNA GRIGORIEVNA: So Nozdryov wasn't lying. . . .

SOFIYA IVANOVNA: No! So Korobochka answers him, reasonably enough, "I can't sell them because they're dead." And he starts yelling, "No they aren't. I'll decide whether they're dead or not."

ANNA GRIGORIEVNA: (*Shuddering.*) My God!

SOFIYA IVANOVNA: In short, he made the most *scandaleuse* commotion and the whole village came on the run—simply an *horreur, horreur, horreur*!. . . . It gave me quite a turn when I heard it, but I said "I have to dash over to Anna Grigorievna and let her know!"

EPISODE 12   85

ANNA GRIGORIEVNA: There must be something to those dead souls after all.

SOFIYA IVANOVNA: Wait, there's more, my dear. This Korobochka says, "He forced me to sign a forged paper and threw fifteen rubles in my face!" The things that go on around here!

ANNA GRIGORIEVNA: (*Gravely.*) Say what you like, Sofiya Ivanovna, but these dead souls means something!

SOFIYA IVANOVNA: (*Surprised despite what she says.*) Just what I was thinking. (*Slowly.*) What do you suppose they mean?

ANNA GRIGORIEVNA: What do you suppose?

SOFIYA IVANOVNA: What do I suppose?

ANNA GRIGORIEVNA: Yes, I'd like to hear your . . . suppositions.

SOFIYA IVANOVNA: Well, I'm not strong on suppositions . . .

(*They sit silently for a moment, thinking hard.*)

ANNA GRIGORIEVNA: (*Rising, inspired.*) Aha! I'll tell you what these dead souls are all about.

(SOFIYA IVANOVNA *sits up straight, her ears pricked up, and perches on the edge of the sofa.*)

GOGOL: Thus a Russian huntsman, drawing near a forest from which a hare is about to emerge, is transformed, all eyes, his sight piercing the murky air . . .

ANNA GRIGORIEVNA: These dead souls are . . .

SOFIYA IVANOVNA: Say it, say it, say it!

ANNA GRIGORIEVNA: These dead souls . . .

SOFIYA IVANOVNA: (*All aquiver.*) Tell me, for heaven's sake!

ANNA GRIGORIEVNA: Are simply camouflage. The truth is that Chichikov is planning to kidnap the Governor's daughter.

SOFIYA IVANOVNA: (*Turns pale and wrings her hands.*) Oh my God! Well, that's something I never would have supposed!

ANNA GRIGORIEVNA: Why, the minute you opened your mouth, I figured out what was what.

SOFIYA IVANOVNA: What are they teaching those hussies in finishing school? Call that innocence?

ANNA GRIGORIEVNA: Innocence, my foot! She's insufferably affected.

SOFIYA IVANOVNA: Oh, Anna Grigorievna, how can you call her affected? She's a graven image and white as chalk!

ANNA GRIGORIEVNA: How can you say that? She wears rouge an inch thick. It was peeling off in strips like plaster. Takes after her mother in that. . . .

SOFIYA IVANOVNA: Anyway, our menfolk must be crazy to see anything in her. And as for our Prince Charming . . . the beast! He positively nauseated me!

ANNA GRIGORIEVNA: Still there were some ladies who gave him a second look.

SOFIYA IVANOVNA: Do you mean me? You can never say that, never, never, never! But there were some ladies, who act so high-and-mighty now . . .

ANNA GRIGORIEVNA: Pardon me! There was nothing *scandaleuse* about my conduct!

SOFIYA IVANOVNA: Why get so snippy? You weren't the only lady who practically crawled all over him.

(*A storm is about to break, but they recollect themselves, take a deep breath, and settle down again.*)

SOFIYA IVANOVNA: Still, how could Chichikov who is, after all, just passing through, have dared? He must have accomplices.

ANNA GRIGORIEVNA: Of course he does!

SOFIYA IVANOVNA: Who, do you suppose?

EPISODE 12

ANNA GRIGORIEVNA: Why, Nozdryov!

SOFIYA IVANOVNA: Really? Nozdryov?

ANNA GRIGORIEVNA: Who else could it be? You know Nozdryov would gamble away his own father at cards.

SOFIYA IVANOVNA: Goodness, what a mine of fascinating information you are! I never would have supposed that Nozdryov was mixed up in it!

ANNA GRIGORIEVNA: I always suspected it.

SOFIYA IVANOVNA: Well I never!

(*The* PUBLIC PROSECUTOR *enters.*)

ANNA GRIGORIEVNA: (*Hurrying up to him.*) Antipatr, can you imagine what Sofiva Ivanovna just told me?

PUBLIC PROSECUTOR: Not . . . bad news, I hope?

SOFIYA IVANOVNA: No, no, don't worry. We simply—I mean, I simply have proof that Chichikov is actually buying dead souls. . . .

PUBLIC PROSECUTOR: (*Alarmed.*) Chichikov is . . . actually . . . buying dead souls . . .

ANNA GRIGORIEVNA: Just to create a diversion, because you know what he's really up to? Oh, the minute Sofiya Ivanovna told me, I knew it all, and I said . . .

PUBLIC PROSECUTOR: Actually buying dead souls?

SOFIYA IVANOVNA: Positively!

PUBLIC PROSECUTOR: As a diversion?

ANNA GRIGORIEVNA: (*In triumph.*) Because he's really planning to kidnap the Governor's daughter!

(SOFIYA IVANOVNA *nods her head furiously in agreement.*)

PUBLIC PROSECUTOR: (*Blinking and flicking snuff from his whiskers with his handkerchief.*) The Governor's dau . . . to acquire more . . .

ANNA GRIGORIEVNA: (*Annoyed.*) No, not to acquire more dead souls! Will you pay attention, you aggravating man! To persuade everyone that it's dead souls and not the Governor's daughter he's after. . . .

(PUBLIC PROSECUTOR *collapses into a chair.*)

SOFIYA IVANOVNA: Come along, Anna Grigorievna, we really must tell Praskoviya Fyodorovna!

GOGOL: It took them a trifle over half an hour to turn the whole town topsy-turvy. The state of the officials was like that of a schoolboy whose chums have shoved a twist of paper filled with snuff up his nose while he is napping. Inhaling all that snuff during a snore, he wakes up, shakes himself, stares about with popping eyes, and cannot guess where he is. Only gradually does he perceive his laughing chums, the morning sun peeping through the window, birdsong in the forest—and only then does he realize he's got a snootful of snuff.

(*The* OFFICIALS *who have entered all sneeze heartily.*)

POSTMASTER: Is this a parable or what? There's no logic to it.

SANITATION INSPECTOR: Only a fool would buy dead souls. What would he buy them with, fairy gold?

CHIEF OF POLICE: But how on earth did the Governor's daughter get mixed up in this? Is he planning to make her a present of the dead souls, or what?

BUREAU CHIEF: What's the world coming to when people spread stories like this? There isn't the least sense to it . . .

PUBLIC PROSECUTOR: There must be some sense to it, or people wouldn't spread it!

(*As* GOGOL *speaks, the stage becomes more and more congested with people weaving in and out, and a steady buzz of gossip is heard.*)

GOGOL: The whole town, which hitherto had seemed dormant, swirled up like a tornado. All the slugabeds crawled out of the woodwork: homebodies who normally couldn't be tempted out by an offer of chowder cooked with sturgeons five feet long emerged from beneath their rocks. (*A very bizarre pair—an immensely tall gangling man and a Russian in a tartan kilt—appear.*) A certain Sysoy Pafnutevich and a certain Macdonald Carlovich whom no one had ever heard of before popped up and became drawing-room fixtures. The main street was crammed with carriages—and the kasha hit the fan.

A CHORUS OF OFFICIALS AND TOWNSFOLK, LADIES AND SERVANTS: (*As a madrigal.*) Dead souls. Governor's daughter. Stuff and nonsense. Poppycock! Horse feathers! Dead souls! Kidnapping! Governor's daughter! Fiddle-dee-dee! Blather! Dead souls! Arrant rubbish! Governor's daughter! Too absurd! Dead souls! Dead souls! (*The madrigal ends in unison with:*) Oh, what the hell!

GOGOL: The townsfolk divided into two schools of thought, diametrically opposed to one another: the masculine and the feminine.

(*The characters divide into two diagonal lines, men and women.*)

ANNA GRIGORIEVNA: Oh, Chichikov's been in love with her for a long time, they'd been meeting in the garden by moonlight.

SOFIYA IVANOVNA: He's simply made of money, so the Governor has nothing against it.

LADY WITH BLUE PLUME: But they can't get married, because Chichikov already has a wife he's deserted and she wrote a touching letter to the Governor, and that's why he has to kidnap the girl.

LADY WITH WHITE PLUME: No, no, no, that's all wrong, he isn't married. What happened was, he decided to start by wooing the mother, but when she found out he was really after her daughter, she had a change of heart and rejected him flat out—and that's why he has to kidnap the girl.

GOVERNOR'S WIFE: What's this I hear! How insulting! How disgraceful! (*Turning on her DAUGHTER.*) How long has this been going on? Where have you been meeting him? What happened in that carriage accident?

GOVERNOR'S DAUGHTER: Boo-hoo! (*Burst into sobs.*)

(*Ladies depart in a flurry.*)

GOVERNOR: Under no circumstances is that man Chichikov to be admitted to my house at any time or on any pretext!

CHIEF OF POLICE: This kidnapping story's all bosh!

SANITATION INSPECTOR: A woman's like a sack: She'll take in anything, carry it around, and then spill it out her mouth.

POSTMASTER: Even so, there's something very fishy going on.

PUBLIC PROSECUTOR: There is indeed! Gentlemen, a new Governor-General has just been appointed! You know what that means!

CHIEF OF POLICE: Shake-ups!

BUREAU CHIEF: Dressing-downs!

POSTMASTER: Rakings over the coals!

PUBLIC PROSECUTOR: Exactly. What if the new Governor-General were to hear these silly rumors? It's not your skin you'd be saving, but your life!

SANITATION INSPECTOR: Good Lord! What if the Governor-General were to think dead souls refer to the patients who died in my infirmary during the epidemic!

PUBLIC PROSECUTOR: Worse yet. What if Chichikov himself is an official sent here by the Governor-General to spy on us?

BUREAU CHIEF: Nonsense. (*Turning pale.*) But what if Chichikov really did buy dead souls? *I* was the one who approved the bill of sale!

POSTMASTER: Oh dear, do you remember that affair in the village of Bickering, when the Rural Police Inspector, who was known to be too fond of visiting the peasants' wives, was found dead on the highway with his face missing? And the court decided he had died of indigestion? Suppose the whole matter gets dredged up again?

GOVERNOR: Gentlemen, I have said nothing heretofore, because I didn't want to alarm you. But I have just received two documents. One of them orders us to instigate a search for a circulator of counterfeit money who is using various aliases and who is thought to be at work in this province.

POSTMASTER: Counterfeit money!

SANITATION INSPECTOR: Do you suppose Chichikov . . .

GOVERNOR: And the other document comes from the Governor of the next province who informs me that a certain highway robber has escaped and that I am to apprehend any suspicious person who has not presented his credentials.

POSTMASTER: Highway robber!

SANITATION INSPECTOR: You don't suppose Chichikov. . . .

PUBLIC PROSECUTOR: He did tell me he had lots of enemies who made attempts on his life.

BUREAU CHIEF: It's unthinkable!

CHIEF OF POLICE: It seems to me, my friends, that the best way to put these rumors to rest is to do some investigating. I propose that we question the parties who are alleged to have sold Chichikov the dead souls.

Episode 13

(*Three chairs are set up under interrogation lights. In one area the* PUBLIC PROSECUTOR *questions a seated* SOBAKEVICH. *In another the* BUREAU CHIEF *questions a seated* KOROBOCHKA. *In the third the seated* CHIEF OF POLICE *questions* SELIFAN *and* PETRUSHKA.)

PUBLIC PROSECUTOR: Might I ask you what kind of serfs you sold to Pavel Ivanovich Chichikov?

SOBAKEVICH: What do you mean, what kind? Good ones! The deed of sale tells you that; why the coachmaker alone—

PUBLIC PROSECUTOR: Still, there are an awful lot of rumors at large in town . . .

SOBAKEVICH: There are an awful lot of idiots at large in town.

BUREAU CHIEF: Tell me, did an individual show up at your house late one night and threaten to kill you if you didn't give him certain souls?

KOROBOCHKA: Fifteen rubles he gave me! Put yourself in my shoes, I'm a poor ignorant widow woman. It's easy to pull the wool over my eyes, kind sir. With hemp, I know the price, and lard—

BUREAU CHIEF: Yes, yes, but tell me as circumstantially as you can, did he have any pistols on his person?

KOROBOCHKA: God preserve me, no, no, pistols. I'm just a poor widow woman, I can't be expected to know what dead souls are fetching these days. Why don't you let me know the real price?

BUREAU CHIEF: What price is that?

KOROBOCHKA: Why, the going price of a dead person these days!

CHIEF OF POLICE: (*To* PETRUSHKA.) Where's that smell coming from? (PETRUSHKA *shrugs, making the smell worse.*) What's your master like?

PETRUSHKA: Like any master.

CHIEF OF POLICE: Who does he associate with?

PETRUSHKA: The better sort of folks. Landowners and officials . . . there was this one Mister Perekroyev . . . (*Puffs in his face.*)

CHIEF OF POLICE: God! (*Throws him out.*)

PUBLIC PROSECUTOR: Mikhail Semyonych, these rumors are very disconcerting: the souls aren't souls, they're going to be resettled, Chichikov is an enigma. According to the tittle-tattle . . .

SOBAKEVICH: Don't be such an old woman!

BUREAU CHIEF: Suppose you show me the banknotes he gave you. Just what was it he bought?

KOROBOCHKA: Yes, he bought from me; but why won't you tell me the going price, kind sir, so's I'll know what dead souls go for?

BUREAU CHIEF: Why do you keep talking prices? Did he try to rape you?

KOROBOCHKA: (*Crosses herself.*) How can you say such a thing! Oh, I see, you're a travelling salesman, too! (*Peers suspiciously at him.*)

CHIEF OF POLICE: (*To* SELIFAN.) What sort of man is your master?

SELIFAN: He ain't dumb. Ever'body respects him 'cause he done his duty by the state.

CHIEF OF POLICE: Where did he work? In what department?

SELIFAN: In the Snivel Service. Handled erections for the gummint.

CHIEF OF POLICE: Which ones?

SELIFAN: That I couldn't say.

PUBLIC PROSECUTOR: Were the souls you sold him, by any chance, dead?

SOBAKEVICH: (*To* PUBLIC PROSECUTOR.) You should be ashamed to come to me with such questions. If you haven't got more horse-sense than that, why bother an honest man. Why not go to those biddies sitting around knitting and cross-examine them about witches? Why not play marbles with the kiddies? And you a public servant! Public nuisance is more like it! When you die, there won't be one decent thing to remember you by! Get going, you mangy hound! (*The* PROSECUTOR *is crushed.*)

BUREAU CHIEF: (*To* KOROBOCHKA.) No, listen, I'm the Chief of the Administrative Bureau . . .

KOROBOCHKA: That's what you say, but you act the same as that other one . . . you want to hoodwink me, too. Don't you try it! I would've sold you feathers at Christmastime, I really would—

BUREAU CHIEF: What do I need feathers for? I'm not buying anything!

KOROBOCHKA: Buying's an honest business. But if we start cheating one another, why, it's a sin in the sight of God!

BUREAU CHIEF: I'm not a buyer, I'm a bureau—I mean, I'm an official!

KOROBOCHKA: God knows what you are. I'm only a poor widow woman. All I know is you want to buy them yourself!

BUREAU CHIEF: Mother, I suggest you see a doctor! You've got a screw loose! (*The* BUREAU CHIEF *is hysterical.*)

CHIEF OF POLICE: (*To* SELIFAN.) What do you know about your master's dealings?

SELIFAN: Well, now he's got three horses. One of 'em was bought about three years ago; the gray nag he swapped for another one, also gray; the third one was bought . . . (*The* POLICE CHIEF *is in a state of nervous collapse.*)

(*The* THREE OFFICIALS *leave their interrogatees, who depart, and meet center.*)

BUREAU CHIEF: What'd you get out of Sobakevich?

PUBLIC PROSECUTOR: He spat up one side of me and down the other. What about the old woman?

BUREAU CHIEF: All she gave me was a headache. And you discovered?

CHIEF OF POLICE: That his name is Pavel Ivanovich Chichikov. I could use a glass of Madeira.

BUREAU CHIEF: And a lox sandwich.

(*They gather to eat snacks and drink Madeira, which are passed round by domestics.*)

PUBLIC PROSECUTOR: He's a respectable man, a former civil servant, and yet he decides to kidnap the Governor's daughter and terrify old ladies at the dead of night—that may describe some young officer in the hussars, but never a civil servant.

BUREAU CHIEF: If he's a civil servant, what's he doing counterfeiting money?

POSTMASTER: (*Entering.*) Gentlemen, I've just found out who the new Governor-General is to be!

ALL: Who?

POSTMASTER: Count Odnozorovsky-Chementinsky!

PUBLIC PROSECUTOR: Oh no!

BUREAU CHIEF: The last word in strictness, the world's shortest temper.

SANITATION INSPECTOR: (*Entering.*) Have you heard who the new Governor-General is to be?

ALL: Yes!

SANITATION INSPECTOR: I'm told that in his last post he ground his underlings to such fine powder there wasn't enough left to sweep up.

BUREAU CHIEF: The Devil brought this Chichikov right on cue!

PUBLIC PROSECUTOR: My head's spinning.

POSTMASTER: It's not as bad as all that, in a manner of speaking. Governor-Generals come and go; but I've been at my old stand now for thirty years.

SANITATION INSPECTOR: (*Angrily.*) It's all very well for you to talk, Ivan Andreich-Sprechen-Sie-Deutsch. The only mischief you can get into is to close the post-office an hour early. Anybody could be a saint in your position!

PUBLIC PROSECUTOR: I've been too lenient. As Public Prosecutor, I always stamped approved on everyone's service record. I should have denounced you all on a weekly basis.

CHIEF OF POLICE: This has gone far enough! Gentlemen, we have got to settle this business before the new Governor-General arrives.

SANITATION INSPECTOR: How?

CHIEF OF POLICE: By decisive action.

BUREAU CHIEF: How?

CHIEF OF POLICE: By arresting Chichikov as a suspicious character.

BUREAU CHIEF: And what if he arrests *us* as suspicious characters?

CHIEF OF POLICE: What do you mean?

BUREAU CHIEF: What if he turns out to be an undercover agent? Buying up "dead souls" when he's really investigating all the deaths listed as "cause unknown"?

SANITATION INSPECTOR: But he's supposed to be a counterfeitor, isn't he?

BUREAU CHIEF: The Devil knows what he is! You can't read it branded on his forehead.

PUBLIC PROSECUTOR: Perhaps he's that highway robber in disguise?

CHIEF OF POLICE: No, no there's nothing very violent in his manner *or* his conversation.

POSTMASTER: (*Suddenly.*) Gentlemen, do you know who this Chichikov is?

ALL: No, who is he?

POSTMASTER: Gentlemen, he is none other than Captain Kopeikin.

ALL: And just who is Captain Kopeikin?

POSTMASTER: (*Taking a pinch of snuff but guardedly keeping the box from the reach of others.*) Captain Kopeikin—why, really, if a writer were to tell his story, it would be a regular epic, in a

EPISODE 13   97

manner of speaking. (*During the narration,* CAPTAIN KOPEIKIN *enters, played by an unrecognizable* GOGOL.) After the campaign of 1812, my dear sirs, a certain Captain Kopeikin was sent home with other wounded men, for he had had an arm and a leg blown off, if you can imagine that, at Krasny or Leipzig or someplace. Well, at that time, no special provisions had been made for disabled veterans, so Captain Kopeikin sees he'll have to get some work, but Devil knows what kind, because only his left arm was . . . uh, left. Anyhow, he sets off for St Petersburg to petition the Tsar for relief: "Having laid down my life and shed my this, that and the other . . ." Well, what with hitching rides on carts and government convoys, gentlemen, he gets to the capital. Now just picture this: A fellow like that, a Captain Kopeikin, lo and behold, lands in, you might call it, a fairy tale Scheherazade, with that whatchacall Nevsky Prospect unrolling before him and spires in the air and bridges suspended the devil's own way—the hanging gardens of Cleopatra, that's what! Trouble was, Captain Kopeikin's whole cash flow was a pocketful of small change, so the best room he could find was in a seedy tavern, ruble a day with cabbage soup and hash thrown in. So he sees he can't hang around long. Turns out the Tsar is in Paris —everybody who was anybody was still abroad—so Kopeikin stumps off to the Prime Minister, because people tell him the Prime Minister heads a kind of Commission. He gets to where the Prime Minister shacks up, nothing but marble and plate-glass windows and a doorknob that was such a work of art you'd have to scrub your hands with a whole bar of soap before you got up the nerve to touch it. And the reception room was chockful of big brass with gold braid and all sorts of scrambled eggs—in short, the crust de la crust. Suddenly a whiff of zephyr, if you know what I mean, blows through the room, everyone shushes everyone else, and enter the Prime Minister, a regular—well, you can imagine! He comes up to Kopeikin and he says, What's your business?" Everyone else is fainting right and left, but Kopeikin plucks up his courage and says:

GOGOL: Well, your Excellency, here's how it is. I've lost an arm and, so to speak, a leg; and I was wondering whether there might not be compensation of some sort, relating to a pension or what-have-you, get me?

POSTMASTER: Well, the Prime Minister sees he's got a timber tootsie and an empty sleeve, so he says, "Come back in a few days!" My Kopeikin leaves in ecstasy, sort of, spends his last ruble on a bottle of wine and some lamb chops, and is even about to accost some English lady on the street—what with his hot blood racing, you know—when he thinks:

GOGOL: No, I'll save that sort of thing for later, when I get my pension!

POSTMASTER: Well, sir, three-four days later, he shows up at the Prime Minister's, who recognizes him right off the bat, and says, "Glad to see you. Afraid you'll have to wait till the Tsar comes back, 'cause I can't make any decisions without him." So Kopeikin stumps off, mad as a scalded poodle, his tail between his legs, thinking:

GOGOL: I'll go back and tell him I'm down to my last crumb; and if you don't help me out now, I'll, in a manner of speaking, starve to death.

POSTMASTER: So he goes back but they keep telling him the Minister's not in. And yet wherever he goes he sees foreigners tucking into truffles and omelets, making his mouth water, and all he gets on his plate is, "Tomorrow!" So Kopeikin barges right in on the Prime Minister, and says, rude like:

GOGOL: I can't wait no longer.

POSTMASTER: Well, this got the Prime Minister's goat and he tried to shake off Kopeikin, but Kopeikin, egged on by hunger, says:

GOGOL: I'm not stirring from this spot till you do something about my pension.

POSTMASTER: Well, you can imagine. What a contrast: the Prime Minister and some Captain Kopeikin! A pot of gold and a zero! The Minister shoots him a glance—if looks could kill!—but Kopeikin stands his ground. "All right," says the Prime Minister, "if you find the cost of living too high in capital, I'll send you back home at government expense!" So they dump Kopeikin, humble servant of God that he is, into a cart.

GOGOL: Well, a free ride, that's not to be sneezed at.

POSTMASTER: Now, after this, all rumors about Captain Kopeikin were sunk in the river of . . . Leaky, I think the poets call it. But this is just where the plot thickens, gentlemen. No more than two months go by when a band of robbers turns up in the Ryazan forest and the Robin Hood of this band is none other than . . .

CHIEF OF POLICE: Hold on, hold on, Ivan Andreich, you said that Captain Kopeikin was missing an arm and a leg, whereas Chichikov—

(GOGOL/KOPEIKIN *vanishes.*)

POSTMASTER: (*Slapping his forehead.*) Am I a veal chop! (*In an apologetic tone.*) Still, the papers say that the English are such mechanical geniuses that they've invented wooden legs worked by a spring that can carry a man so far he'll never be found.

SANITATION INSPECTOR: *Too* far! You're going to far, Ivan Andreich! Next thing you know you'll be saying Chichikov is Napoleon!

PUBLIC PROSECUTOR: (*As light dawns.*) Napoleon?

BUREAU CHIEF: Come to think of it, haven't you seen those cartoons in the papers? John Bull with Napoleon on a leash, telling Russia they'll let him loose if things don't go right.

POSTMASTER: True enough! England's jealous of Russia's size and might. They might let Boney off St. Helena to sneak back here and stir up trouble.

PUBLIC PROSECUTOR: (*To* CHIEF OF POLICE.) You saw Napoleon in the last campaign, do you think there's a resemblance?

CHIEF OF POLICE: Well, if you turn them sideways, Chichikov's profile does bear a striking resemblance to Napoleon's. And their builds are about the same—not too stout, not too thin.

SANITATION INSPECTOR: So you think Napoleon's roaming around Russia disguised as Chichikov?

PUBLIC PROSECUTOR: *If* he *is* Chichikov!

CHIEF OF POLICE: Let's not let our imaginations run away with us. I sent for Nozdryov, who was the first one to mention dead souls. He seems to be a bosom chum of Chichikov and he's bound to know something about his life.

BUREAU CHIEF: But Nozdryov's such a liar!

CHIEF OF POLICE: We're clutching at straws, aren't we? (*Calls.*) Would you step in here, please, Mr. Nozdryov?

(NOZDRYOV *enters, annoyed.*)

NOZDRYOV: This had better be important. I was watching my servant scrub my puppy's belly-button when you sent for me. He's got to soap it with a special brush three times a day. Where's the card game you mentioned?

CHIEF OF POLICE: In a minute, in a minute. First, we'd appreciate it if you'd tell us all you know about this Chichikov?

NOZDRYOV: (*Very assured.*) Chichikov? That twat! I sold him some dead souls, several thousands worth. Why not?

PUBLIC PROSECUTOR: Then there really were . . .

CHIEF OF POLICE: (*Impatiently.*) Do you happen to know if Chichikov's in this area on a special assignment . . .

POSTMASTER: (*Interrupting.*) As a spy!

NOZDRYOV: Of course, Chichikov's a spy. Why even in school where we were classmates, he was a stool-pigeon. The other kids used to call him Snitchikov, and once they beat him up and his mama had to put two hundred and forty leeches on his nose.

EPISODE 13

CHIEF OF POLICE: Two hundred and forty?

NOZDRYOV: Forty—the two hundred was a slip of the tongue. Oh, yes, he's a spy all right. Where's the cards?

PUBLIC PROSECUTOR: (*Trying to sound unconcerned.*) And . . . and what do you think of the rumor that Chichikov is passing counterfeit money?

NOZDRYOV: Of course Chichikov's passing counterfeit money. He had two million phoney rubles stashed under his bed; but when the government sealed the doors and stationed guards around the house, Chichikov did a switch the next day and all the authorities found was real money. Pretty cute, huh?

BUREAU CHIEF: Oh, my God.

PUBLIC PROSECUTOR: (*Stammering.*) Now . . . about . . . about . . . the notion that Chichikov may be planning to k-k-k-kidnap . . .

NOZDRYOV: The Governor's daughter? Of course, he's planning to kidnap the Governor's daughter!

CHIEF OF POLICE: And is it a fact that you are personally implicated in this affair, to the extent of aiding and abetting Chichikov?

NOZDRYOV: Of course. If it wasn't for me, it would never come off. I gave Chichikov my own carriage and had relays of fresh horses ready every stage of the way. Let's see, the marriage ceremony was going to be performed by Father Sidor: He charges seventy-five rubles, but I got him to lower the price by threatening to turn him in for marrying Mikhailo the grain merchant to Mikhailo's own godmother, which, as you know, the law regards as incest. Now let's see, the names of the drivers were . . .

CHIEF OF POLICE: All right, all right, that'll do. (*He is clearly fed up, but his less experienced colleagues are beginning to fall apart.*) "Pull and pull and pull, you won't get milk from a bull."

PUBLIC PROSECUTOR: But do you have any theory as to who . . . who . . .

NOZDRYOV: Who Chichikov is? Well, I've been wondering . . .

PUBLIC PROSECUTOR: Don't tell me you think he's Napoleon!

(*The* CHIEF OF POLICE *gestures to the* PUBLIC PROSECUTOR *to shut up, but it's too late.*)

NOZDRYOV: Is Chichikov Napoleon? (*Pregnant pause.*) To tell the truth, that hadn't occurred to me, but now that I think of it . . .

PUBLIC PROSECUTOR: B-b-but . . . Napoleon grew up in France, and you told us you w-w-went to school with Chichikov . . .

NOZDRYOV: Of course Napoleon grew up in France, but then Chichikov was absent from school a lot. And he never explained why, even to me, his oldest friend. And a couple of years back there was this prophet who got jailed for slander, 'cause he said that Napoleon was Antichrist and was kept on a chain of stone in a dungeon six walls thick but would one day break his chain and conquer the world. Now if you take the name Napoleon and give each letter its numerical value, and then you take the name Chichikov . . .

PUBLIC PROSECUTOR: Then Chichikov is ah . . . ah . . . ah . . .

CHIEF OF POLICE: That's quite enough, Nozdryov!

PUBLIC PROSECUTOR: A-a-antichrist!

NOZDRYOV: Well, I don't know about Antichrist, but he's certainly a tame twat!

(*The* PUBLIC PROSECUTOR *falls bang! off the chair, flat on his back.*)

OFFICIALS: (*Clustering round him, panicky.*) Oh my God! What is it!

CHIEF OF POLICE: (*Lifting the* PUBLIC PROSECUTOR*'s wrist.*) He's dead. (*A Russian Orthodox requiem plays faintly under the next speech.*)

GOGOL: And so the Public Prosecutor's colleagues found out that he had a soul, although he had never flaunted it. A man who but a little while ago had been playing whist and blinking his left eye beneath his bushy eyebrows was now laid out on a table, with one eyebrow still upraised in a questioning manner. What the deceased was asking about, why he had lived or died, God alone knows.

(*The* PUBLIC PROSECUTOR *has been laid out on top of the table, and the* OFFICIALS, *holding lighted candles, kneel around it during the next scene.*)

SOBAKEVICH'S VOICE: When you die, there won't be one decent thing to remember you by!

Episode 14

GOGOL: Meanwhile, our indisposed hero was entirely unaware of what was going on. He spent his time gargling milk and fig juice, and reading an odd volume of *The Three Musketeers*.

(CHICHIKOV, *in a dressing gown, gets out of bed and sits down to tea, when the door flies open and* NOZDRYOV *pops in.*)

NOZDRYOV: You know the saying, "Seven miles out of the way for a friend is not out of the way!" (*Takes off his cap.*) I was just passing by, saw a light in your window, thought "I'll drop in." Ah, tea, great. (*Takes* CHICHIKOV*'s cup.*) Tell your servant to fill me a pipe.

CHICHIKOV: (*Drily.*) I don't smoke.

NOZDRYOV: Pish-tush. You smoke like a chimney. Hey Vakhramey!

CHICHIKOV: His name's not Vakhramey, it's Petrushka.

NOZDRYOV: What? Didn't you use to have a Vakhramey?

CHICHIKOV: Never.

NOZDRYOV: That's right, it's Derebin who's got Vakhramey. Say, old boy, why have you been so out of touch the last few days? Deep into scientific studies, you bookworm? I was playing cards with Perependev a while back and he says, "If only Chichikov was here, it's just his sort of thing . . ."

CHICHIKOV: I don't know any Perependev.

NOZDRYOV: Piffle! Of course you do. By the way, I don't bear you any grudge for that dirty trick with the checkers the other day. I'm too easy-going . . . Oh, incidentally, the whole town's turned against you. They say you're printing counterfeit money, but I stood up for you and told them about our schooldays together.

CHICHIKOV: (*Bounding out of his chair.*) Counterfeit money!

NOZDRYOV: You scared them plenty! They figure you for a highway robber and an undercover agent. . . . The Public Prosecutor was so scared he cashed in his chips—funeral's this afternoon. You going? Tell the truth, I didn't think you had it in you to pull off something that risky—

CHICHIKOV: (*Cagily.*) Something *what* risky?

NOZDRYOV: Kidnapping the governor's daughter. Although I expected it, by God, when I saw the way the two of you were carrying on at the ball. Pity you picked her, though; she's a waste of time. Now you take that niece of Vikussov's, there's a real piece!

CHICHIKOV: What are you talking about? Are you raving? (*Eyes bulge from his head.*) Kidnapping the governor's daughter?

NOZDRYOV: Oh, don't act so hush-hush! I'm here to help you. I'll supply the coach and bribe the priest, but listen, you've got to lend me three thousand rubles! It's a matter of life or death!

CHICHIKOV: You come here, proclaim that I'm printing counterfeit money, kidnapping the governor's daughter, causing the prosecutor's death, and then you have the

EPISODE 14

audacity to . . . to . . . why, if what you say has even a . . . grain of truth in it . . . if the whole town *is* talking . . . it must be your fault, because at every conceivable opportunity you were shouting about your friend Chichikov this and your friend Chichikov that . . . Well, your friend Chichikov has had it up to here, and if you don't get the hell out . . . When my respectability and honor are impugned . . . (*He rushes at* NOZDRYOV, *who retreats.*)

NOZDRYOV: Well, if I'd known you'd get so upset . . . (*Leaves, but sticks his head in again.*) Make it twenty rubles?

CHICHIKOV: Out!

NOZDRYOV: You can't take it with you! And the next time a friend comes calling for a measly ten rubles, you ought to let him have it, even if you are involved in scientific research!

(CHICHIKOV *flings a boot at his head, and he disappears.*)

CHICHIKOV: (*Shouts.*) Selifan! Petrushka!

PETRUSHKA: (*Enters.*) Right away, Pavel Ivanovich!

CHICHIKOV: For God's sake, open a window! No, start packing! We're going to leave.

(PETRUSHKA *pulls out the trunk, wiping the dust from his hands on his coat; he and* CHICHIKOV *start dumping everything into it: socks, dirty linen, clean linen, boot-trees, a calendar, just as they come to hand.* SELIFAN *very slowly shuffles into the room.*)

CHICHIKOV: We're leaving. Have the carriage ready, grease the wheels, harness the horses, in two hours' time. Understand?

SELIFAN: (*Slowly scratching his neck.*) Yes, but, Pavel Ivanovich, the horses got to be shod.

CHICHIKOV: You pork roast! You birdbrain! Why didn't you say so before? Didn't you have the time?

SELIFAN: Plenty o' time . . . But that there iron rim on the front wheel ain't gonna hold. Two more relays with these hard rains and it'll snap right off.

CHICHIKOV: (*Wringing his hands, walks up to* SELIFAN *so ferociously that the driver backs off to one side.*) You bastard! You want to murder me, do you, you cutthroat, you sea serpent! Eh? Eh? Three weeks we've been in this godforsaken hole, eh? And not one word from you, you shiftless lout—only now, at the last minute, you pull a stunt like this! You knew it all the time, didn't you? Eh? Eh?

SELIFAN: (*Hanging his head.*) You kin flog me if you want.

CHICHIKOV: No time for that! Get a move on. Fetch blacksmiths and have everything done in two hours. And if it isn't ready, I'll bend *you* into a horseshoe with my bare hands.

SELIFAN: (*Gets to the door, turns 'round.*) And another thing, boss, that dapple-gray better be sold. He's a low-down critter, boss, the orneriest brute there is . . .

CHICHIKOV: Stop lecturing me, you fool! If things aren't ready in two hours I'll give you such a beating you won't recognize your own face in the mirror. Now scram!

GOGOL: But all things come to an end, and within five and a half hours of fuming and fretting, the carriage was harnessed and, after such a long stay in the town you must all be fed up with, it rolled out the gates of the inn.

CHICHIKOV: (*Crossing himself; in the carriage.*) Thank God!

(*Requiem swells up. The* OFFICIALS *have lifted the table-top as if it were a coffin and are bearing the* PUBLIC PROSECUTOR *to the cemetery in procession led by the* PRIEST. SELIFAN, *piously doffing his hat, stops the carriage;* PETRUSHKA *also uncovers.*)

CHICHIKOV: (*In the carriage.*) So the Public Prosecutor lived until he up and died! And now the papers will print that a respected citizen and exemplary husband and father has departed this life to the bereavement of all humanity and similar nonsense! When the truth is you amounted to little more than your bushy eyebrows! Still, they say meeting a funeral is good luck. (*To* SELIFAN.) Drive on!

Episode 15

GOGOL: Eventually, the cobbled street ended, the tollgate was passed, and Chichikov was again on his travels. Mile after mile of highway with drab villages, ramshackle towns, bridges undergoing repairs, fields so vast the eye could not take them in, shuffling tramps, soldiers on horseback, a plaintive song in the distance, the pealing of church-bells, and an endless horizon . . . (*A plangent folk song—like "Polyushka" begins quietly in the background.*) Russia! Russia! From this beautiful remote foreign spot I see thee now. Everything about thee is desolate, bare and flat, thy towns strewn over thy plains like fly-specks. Thou hast no spectacular scenery, no marvels of art to enchant the eye. Then, what is that mysterious power that draws me to thee? What is there in thy plaintive song that appeals and sobs and clutches at my very heart? Russia, what is the bond between us? Here I stand, my mind benumbed by thy vastness. What does that unimaginable expanse portend? Is it not space for a titan to stretch his legs as a flower opens to the sun? Ah, what a wondrous, dazzling horizon the world wots little of! Russia! My Russia! . . .

CHICHIKOV: (*To* SELIFAN.) Whoa! Whoa, you nitwit! Are you running away with us?

SELIFAN: Sorry, boss! I allus git carried away when we're on the open road.

GOGOL: The road! A sunny day, autumn leaves, a nip in the air . . . A tempting drowsiness steals upon you . . .

LUIGI: *Ma, Signor* Gogol, before you take nap, tell me: who is Chichikov? Is Napoleone Buonaparte, no?

GOGOL: Hardly. I'm afraid you don't admire my hero. Luigi?

LUIGI: Is no right, theese hero. A hero should be a *paladino*, beautiful and full of de virtue.

GOGOL: Well, I admit Chichikov's corpulence is against him. And as for virtue, I might get around to such a hero in time, but now? Virtuous heroes are six a penny, they should be given a rest, nobody takes them seriously. No, it's time to put a scoundrel center stage! And Chichikov is a scoundrel.

LUIGI: Eef only 'e could be scoundrel king or *Milord Ladro*?

GOGOL: Alas, no, Chichikov's origins were obscure and humble, though he didn't favor either of his parents. The midwife, of the breed known as runts, remarked at his birth:

MIDWIFE: (*Pulling a baby from the carriage.*) He didn't come out the way I thought! He should resemble his grandmother on his mother's side, but as the saying goes, "Not like mother, not like dad, He's like a passing beggar lad."

GOGOL: From the beginning, life scowled sourly on him, for he had no friends or playmates, and his world was defined by his elders. His father . . .

CHICHIKOV'S FATHER: (*A coughing consumptive, shuffling around and spitting into a square spitoon.*) Write a hundred times "Tell No Lies," "Obey Your Elders," "Cherish Virtue in your Heart." (*The child* CHICHIKOV *scrapes away with his pen.*) And no nonsense!

GOGOL: He was sent to school:

CHICHIKOV'S FATHER: Now remember, Pavlusha: study hard, don't get into mischief, and don't act like a fool. And above all, please your teachers and superiors, and you'll go to the head of the class. Don't get too friendly with your schoolmates, they'll be the first to betray you if you're in trouble. And most important, save your money: Money's the best friend you have, it can do anything!

GOGOL: His teacher:

CHICHIKOV'S TEACHER: I don't put up with impertinence! (*As he thrashes* CHICHIKOV) Aptitude and talent is so much hogwash! What I look for in a boy is conduct. You may not known your capital *A* from a hole in the ground, still, if you behave properly, you'll get high marks. But if you're a genius and you act snotty, it's a zero every time.

EPISODE 15

GOGOL: That was one lesson Chichikov took to heart and when he left school, he received a diploma inscribed in gold:

CHICHIKOV'S TEACHER: For Exemplary Diligence amd Good Behavior.

GOGOL: His father died leaving him only this piece of advice:

CHICHIKOV'S FATHER: Save (*cough*) every (*cough*) penny! (*Wheeze.*) (*Expires.*)

GOGOL: And so when his teacher was dismissed for some reason and took to drink and was starving to death, and his schoolmates made up a collection, only Pavlushka Chichikov, the prize pupil, gave nothing.

CHICHIKOV'S TEACHER: (*Weeping bitterly.*) And he was so well-behaved! Never a troublemaker, smooth as silk! He put one over on me. . . .

GOGOL: Not that Chichikov loved money for its own sake. Instead, he pictured a future life of ease, full of good things: carriages, a comfortable house, tasty dinners, a loving wife — and so every penny was set aside for the time to come. With difficulty, he got a post as clerk in the Treasury Department and set to work with great assiduity. But his immediate Superior was a man of implacable stoniness, with nothing human about him. His face was of marble, so pitted and pimply that the Devil must have threshed peas on it.

CHICHIKOV: (*Obsequiously.*) Do let me clean out your inkwell, sir, and cut you a new quill.

SUPERIOR: Hmph!

CHICHIKOV: I've brushed your coat and cap; the whitewash on the wall got on them.

SUPERIOR: Hmph!

CHICHIKOV: Excuse me, sir, but I happened to see you at church last Sunday with your daughter. What a handsome young lady!

SUPERIOR: (*Pause; smile.*) Come and have tea.

GOGOL: The superior's elderly daughter also had a face that the Devil had been threshing peas on. For a while Chichikov courted her and acted like her fiancé, but as soon as he got a promotion with his superior's backing, he dropped them.

SUPERIOR: He put one over on me, that limb of Satan. . . .

GOGOL: To every client who put his hand in his pocket to offer him a bribe, Chichikov would say:

CHICHIKOV: No, no! (*Smiling.*) How can you think that I would ever . . . ! No, just doing my duty. Rest assured, this business will be dealt with by tomorrow. Let me know where you're staying, and I'll see that the papers are delivered.

CLIENT: What a man—a pearl beyond price!

GOGOL: But after a three day's wait:

CHICHIKOV: You really must forgive us! We were simply swamped! Tomorrow, I promise!

GOGOL: But after another three days:

CLIENT: What's going on?

CHICHIKOV: Well, you see you have to give something to the clerks.

CLIENT: Well, why not? I'm prepared to divide a couple of rubles among them.

CHICHIKOV: Each one has to get twenty-five rubles.

CLIENT: Twenty-five rubles for each of those pen-pushers!

CHICHIKOV: Don't get so worked up: The pen-pushers will get a few kopeks apiece, the rest goes to their superiors!

CLIENT: In the old days, you used to hand the boss a ten-ruble note and that was that. Now, with all this refinement and sophistication, it takes a week before you catch on. . . . He put one over on me, that smooth-talking grafter!

GOGOL: Gradually a little nest-egg began building, and Chichikov went in for clean linen and fancy soap and eau de

EPISODE 15   111

Cologne. But there came a new Bureau Chief, a military man who set his face against all abuses, as he called them. And, as luck would have it, at just this time, Chichikov offended one of his colleagues by calling him,

CHICHIKOV: You son of a priest!

GOGOL: Which, in fact, he was. But this colleague was so insulted that he denounced Chichikov secretly, and the thunderbolt broke over both their heads. (*A clap of thunder ejects Chichikov from his carriage. He rolls on the ground.*) Both officials were arrested, their worldly goods confiscated, and they perished. That is, the colleague lay down and died; but Chichikov had somehow had the presence of mind to secrete some of his money, and through flattery, bribery, and general all-round expertise, he managed to retain—

CHICHIKOV: Ten measly thousand, two dozen linen shirts, a carriage, and two serfs. Oh yes, and six cakes of scented soap.

GOGOL: Give credit where credit is due, to his indomitable strength of character! His patience! His industry!

CHICHIKOV: Why me? Why has this disaster come crashing down on me? What government employee doesn't feather his nest? I never robbed widows and orphans; I merely took advantage of surpluses, taking what anybody would. Why must I perish like a squashed worm? And what will my children say of me? "Our father was a lousy bastard, he didn't leave us a thing!"

GOGOL: Chichikov had no children, but he was always concerned about future offspring. And so, waiting for something to turn up, girding his loins against humiliation, he became a legal agent, looked down on by bureaucrats and clerks alike. He cooled his heels in waiting-rooms and crawled on his belly like a reptile, for the sake of a few clients. One of his clients had an estate in the last stages of disintegration.

CHICHIKOV: Cattle killed off by hoof-and-mouth, crops failed, overseers stole the profits, workers died in the epidemic, and now the owner's starving to death. The only thing left, Mr. Secretary, is to mortgage the serfs. And my client is afraid . . .

SECRETARY: I realize, Mr. Chichikov, that mortgaging property to the government is a new experience for most landowners. There's really nothing to fear. (Oh, by the way, thank you for that bottle of Madeira.)

CHICHIKOV: Don't mention it. No, my client is afraid that he won't get much money because half his serfs died off in the last epidemic . . .

SECRETARY: Why? Aren't they listed on the Census Bureau's tax-rolls?

CHICHIKOV: Yes, they are. He still pays taxes on them.

SECRETARY: Then what's there to worry about? You know the saying, "Death is death, and birth is birth; and each one has its special worth."

CHICHIKOV: I don't quite follow. . . .

SECRETARY: : One peasant dies, another gets born, no one's the loser. So long as these peasants exist on paper, the Government will assume them to be alive, and your client can use them as collateral.

CHICHIKOV: (*Smacking his forehead.*) I'm a four-star idiot! What an idea! If it was a snake, it'd bite me!

SECRETARY: I beg your pardon?

CHICHIKOV: Nothing, sorry.

SECRETARY: (*Leaving.*) Tell your client to leave it to me.

CHICHIKOV: (*To himself.*) If I were to buy all those souls that have died, before the new census is taken. . . . Say I manage to get a thousand of them, and I mortgage them to the Government for two hundred rubles a soul, why, I'd have a fortune of two hundred thousand right there! And now's the time for it, what with the epidemic. Lots of peasants have died off, thank God! It gets harder to pay the taxes every year. Somebody might even pay me to take them off his hands! Selifan! Petrushka!

SELIFAN: Boss?

CHICHIKOV: Harness the horses! We're going to take a trip into the country! (*To himself.*) Country! Land! You can't legally mortgage peasants without land. I know! I'll say I'm buying them to resettle them. That can be done right through the courts. (*To* PETRUSHKA.) Don't forget to pack my soap!

PETRUSHKA: And a couple of loaves of bread?

CHICHIKOV: Of course. (*To himself.*) It's not going to be easy, and there's always the danger of a scandal. But that's what God gave man his intelligence for. (*Chuckling as he gets into the brichka.*) And the best part is nobody will believe it, it's too improbable. No one will ever believe this is for real.

(*The brichka starts out again.*)

GOGOL: So you see, Luigi, if Chichikov had never come up with this scheme, my epic would never have been born.

LUIGI: Is all his fault then, signore?

GOGOL: Do you think it was all *my* invention?

LUIGI: Is still a *ladro*, signore!

GOGOL: A scoundrel, you say? Why be so severe? If he ordered a drink at this café, you'd be polite to him, you'd serve him, and you'd simply call him a businessman. But because he is the hero of an epic, he's a scoundrel?

LUIGI: Si, si, signore, but is much nicer things in life to write about.

GOGOL: Just you wait, mio caro Luigi. Direct a searching gaze at a man and he'll change before your very eyes. Perhaps, even now, in Chichikov's heart of hearts, a passion not of his own choosing is drawing him to great deeds, and his sterile existence may yet prostrate a man before the wisdom of heaven. Who knows?

CHICHIKOV: Hey, Selifan! What are you up to now?

SELIFAN: (*Slowly.*) Huh?

CHICHIKOV: You nincompoop! You call that driving? Give those horses a taste of the whip!

SELIFAN: Righto! Giddap, me hearties! Don't be scairt! Fly along, me birdies!

GOGOL: Ah, thou troika-bird! Only a spirited people could have called thee into being, not cunningly contrived but slapped together by a peasant with an axe! The driver cracks his whip, breaks into song, and his steeds speed away like a whirlwind, the road quaking beneath them, and the troika soars higher and higher and higher, churning up the dust and swirling through the air. (*During this speech, the entire cast composes the troika.*) And art not thou, my Russia, soaring along like a spirited, unovertakeable troika? What means this headlong rush, so terror-inspiring? And what unknown power impels those steeds, whose like the world knows not? Ah, those steeds, those steeds, what steeds they are! With whirlwinds seated in their manes! Have your sharp ears heard the familiar song from on high? (*The harness-bells begin to turn into Rostov chimes, and the coachman's song swells into a mighty chorus.*) You strain your brazen chests and, barely grazing the earth with your hooves, you cleave the air in one unbroken line, and the troika, inspired by God, whirls onward . . . whither, oh whither art thou soaring, Russia? Give me thine answer!

[END]

www.ingramcontent.com/pod-product-compliance
Lightning Source LLC
Chambersburg PA
CBHW071709040426
42446CB00011B/1980